The
Presidents
Tidbits & Trivia

Sid Frank & Arden Davis Melick

GREENWICH HOUSE
Distributed by Crown Publishers, Inc.
New York

THE PRESIDENTS

ACKNOWLEDGMENTS

The publisher is very grateful to Dover Publications, Inc., for permission to use illustrations from several publications in the Dover Pictorial Archive Series: *The American Revolution, A Picture Sourcebook,* by John Grafton, *Early Advertising Art,* by Clarence P. Hornung, *Chinese Cut-Paper Designs,* selected by Theodore Menten, *Decorative Silhouettes of the Twenties,* selected by Jo Anne C. Day, *Harter's Picture Archive for Collage and Illustration,* edited by Jim Harter, *1800 Woodcuts by Thomas Bewick and His School,* edited by Blanche Cirker, *200 Decorative Title-Pages,* edited by Alexander Nesbitt.

We acknowledge with thanks the cooperation of the Heritage Conservation and Recreation Service and the National Park Service, both of the Department of Interior, and the National Archives and various presidential libraries under the General Services Administration for their help in obtaining important information and photographs.

We also wish to thank the Chicago Historical Society for the illustration on page 118; Library of Congress for illustrations on pages 8, 9, 17 top, 20, 21, 24 top, 30 top, 46 top left and right, 47 bottom, 58 bottom left, 62, 64, 78 all, 79 all, 80 top left, 81 top, 82, 83, 89 bottom, 97 bottom, 100 bottom, 101 top, 105 bottom, 109 bottom, 112 center left, 113 top, 114 top and bottom, 121, 122 left, 124, 125, 138 left; New York Public Library Picture Collection for illustrations on pages 10 top, 13 top, 16 bottom, 22, 25, 28 bottom, 43 center, 44 top, 46 bottom, 48 top left, 49 top, 50 left, 52 bottom right, 59 bottom, 63 top, 87 both, 89 top, 96 top right, 113 bottom, 115 bottom, 131 bottom right; Richmond Times Dispatch for cartoon by Seibel on page 45, and Rockwell Inc., for the "old" Life magazine illustration used on page 95.

Book design and initialed illustrations by Dwight Dobbins.
Picture portfolio *Presidents in Focus* designed by Lucille Y. Chomowicz.
Book Editor: Ernest J. Dupuy

The presidential recipes included in this book are from *A Taste of White House Cooking,* by Arden Davis Melick, published by Hammond Incorporated © Copyright 1975, 1977.

This 1984 edition is published by Greenwich House, a division of Arlington House, Inc., distributed by Crown Publishers, Inc., by arrangement with Hammond Incorporated.

Manufactured in the United States of America

Library of Congress Cataloging in Publication Data
Frank, Sid.
    The presidents, tidbits & trivia.
    Includes index.
    1. Presidents—United States—Miscellanea.
I. Melick, Arden Davis.   II. Title.   III. Title:
Presidents, tidbits, and trivia.
E176.1.F789   1984   973'.09'92   84-4052
ISBN: 0-517-385929
n m l k j i h g

Tidbits & Trivia

FROM THE AUTHORS

People have asked me who my favorite President is, and I find it an easy question to answer. My favorite President is Zachary Taylor. Why Zachary Taylor? Because Old Zach was just a plain straight guy who had his faults and made mistakes and got to be President. We all know the Presidency had its George and Tom and Abe and Teddy, but we sometimes forget Zach Taylor. Interesting men, the Presidents. Some great. Some so-so. Some terrible. But all interesting. Well, almost all. I must confess it, I couldn't get very excited about No. 11, Jim Polk.

In this book are tidbits and trivia about Presidents. A tidbit is a tasty morsel. Those we have. Trivia we also have. The trivia deals with the unimportant things about the Presidents . . . the funny things they said, what they ate, their families, relatives, pets, weddings, their horoscopes, what they wore, how they felt about their job, their problems. Come to think of it, just how unimportant are these unimportant things?

There's an odd lot of characters here, like Lemonade Lucy, Old Tippecanoe, the Rose of Long Island, the little Magician, Uncle Jumbo and Emily Spinach. Come and meet them. These are really their stories, not mine.

Sid Frank

. . . .

Like most Americans, I have a long standing affair of the heart with our First Families. My feelings for those who have occupied the White House are quite nonpartisan, but the inner me usually turns to the wives of the Presidents. My heart aches with compassion, pride and admiration for Eleanor Roosevelt. I easily recall stories of the good sports, such as Edith Roosevelt and Bess Truman. Lyndon's Lady Bird charmed me when we met, just as did Betty Ford. Rosalynn Carter astonished me with the depth of her commitment to the goals of her husband — but I was equally impressed with her beauty.

Do I have a favorite? Yes, but there are two of them, both extraordinary persons. The first, Abigail Adams, remembered for hanging clothes to dry in the East Room, more importantly gave a husband, a son, and her own considerable intellect to the cause of the fledgling America. The other, Dolley Madison, linked in name with ice cream, showed courage when the British tried to destroy the Capital. Her pluck and vitality kept Washington, D.C., alive. May their names continue to be remembered and used — even if for the wrong reasons.

Arden Davis Melick

THE PRESIDENTIAL OATH

I do solemnly swear* (or affirm)

that I will faithfully execute

the office of President

of the United States,

and will to the best of my ability,

preserve, protect and defend the

Constitution of the United States.

*Franklin Pierce, inaugurated on Friday, March 4, 1853,
was the only President who did not swear. He affirmed.

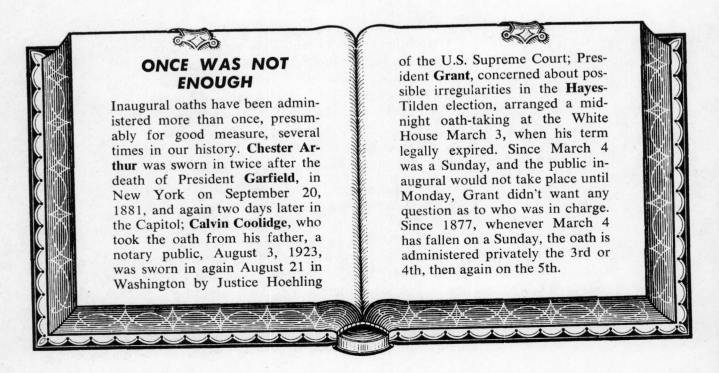

ONCE WAS NOT ENOUGH

Inaugural oaths have been administered more than once, presumably for good measure, several times in our history. **Chester Arthur** was sworn in twice after the death of President **Garfield**, in New York on September 20, 1881, and again two days later in the Capitol; **Calvin Coolidge**, who took the oath from his father, a notary public, August 3, 1923, was sworn in again August 21 in Washington by Justice Hoehling of the U.S. Supreme Court; President **Grant**, concerned about possible irregularities in the **Hayes**-Tilden election, arranged a midnight oath-taking at the White House March 3, when his term legally expired. Since March 4 was a Sunday, and the public inaugural would not take place until Monday, Grant didn't want any question as to who was in charge. Since 1877, whenever March 4 has fallen on a Sunday, the oath is administered privately the 3rd or 4th, then again on the 5th.

THE PRESIDENTS

SOME FAMILY TREE

It wasn't enough that **Franklin D. Roosevelt** claimed kin to more *Mayflower* descendants than any other President, he was also apparently related to more Presidents. Genealogists have traced blood or marriage relationships between FDR and eleven first families, including **Washington, Adams, Madison, John Quincy Adams, Van Buren, William Henry Harrison, Taylor, Grant, Benjamin Harrison, Theodore Roosevelt** and **Taft.**

MAN OF OPPOSITES

He had been born in a log cabin, but he lived in an impressive mansion when he entertained Lincoln in 1861. He could barely read and write at 20, yet at 62 he was chancellor of a major university. Born of poor, hard-working parents, he was apprenticed to a clothmaker as a youth, but before he was 30 he was a prosperous lawyer moving with the most distinguished families. He began his public career as an Anti-Mason, one that opposed secret societies; twenty-seven years later he joined the secret rites of the Order of the Star-Spangled Banner, an anti-Catholic, anti-foreigner fraternal order. As a Whig Congressman he showed strong leadership and vote-getting ability, but he was said to lack personal ambition. In 1844 he ran for governor of New York, and he was nominated and elected Vice-President in 1848. On the day of his inauguration after the death of President Taylor, he said he would not seek re-election. Nonetheless, he actively sought the presidency twice, losing his party's nomination in 1852 and running a poor third as the Know-Nothings' candidate in 1856. **Millard Fillmore** was not your run-of-the-mill President.

JFK TO LBJ

Relations between President **Kennedy** and his second-in-command, **Lyndon Johnson**, were not always peaches and cream.

Composing a birthday telegram to Johnson as a gesture of goodwill, Kennedy said, "This is worse than drafting a state document."

THE FIRST

The first President to receive a transcontinental telegram was **Abraham Lincoln,** in 1861.

THANKS, MA

A very long time before **Lyndon Johnson** became President, he was a bootblack. During this period, his father bought a local newspaper. While her husband was away on a business trip, Lyndon's mother was in charge of the newspaper. The boy asked her if he could take an ad in the newspaper to promote his bootblack business. She agreed, and it was done.

When Father found out about the ad he didn't say much one way or the other. Not much, except for telling everyone he met, "I bought a newspaper for my wife to advertise that my son is a bootblack."

THE PRESIDENTS

WHO WAS THAT LADY?

Frances Folsom Cleveland, widow of the President, became the first President's wife to remarry when she wed Princeton University Professor Thomas Preston, Jr.

Always popular in political circles, she was accorded great respect as the former First Lady throughout her long life. Accordingly, she was given the seat of honor next to **Dwight D. Eisenhower** on a visit to Princeton. Turning to the General, the elderly former President's wife told him she missed Washington very much indeed.

"Really?" Ike is said to have replied, having no idea who the aged Mrs. Preston might be, "Where did you live?"

WELL, THAT'S THE WAY IT GOES

An old friend from childhood days paid a call on **Dwight Eisenhower** at the White House.

Conversation turned to reminiscence and his friend remembered that Eisenhower's boyhood dream had been to become a famous baseball star.

"And you," said Eisenhower, "wanted to be President of the United States."

His friend nodded. "That's right."

"Well," said Ike, "it looks like neither of us got his wish."

WE'LL LIVE AT MY PLACE

Frank Folsom married Uncle Cleve.

Oh, no, it wasn't that sort of thing at all, although it did have its unusual aspects.

"Frank" was what he called her. Her name was Frances, and she was 21, beautiful, poised and intelligent.

Uncle Cleve was what she called him. Her late father's ex-law partner, her guardian, 49 years old, and President of the United States, his name was Grover.

MY FATHER TAUGHT ME ALL I KNOW

Three Presidents were the sons of ministers. They were **Chester A. Arthur, Grover Cleveland** and **Woodrow Wilson**. William Arthur was a Baptist minister; Richard F. Cleveland and Joseph Wilson were Presbyterian clergymen.

When Grover Cleveland was asked why he hadn't married before, he would reply, "I was waiting for my wife to grow up."

At their White House wedding ceremony, which took place in the Blue Room, the President promised to love, honor, comfort, and keep Frances, but not "obey."

The happy couple, and they were, occupied the Executive Mansion for the remaining three years of his term. When Benjamin Harrison defeated Cleveland for re-election, they moved out. Before they did, however, they gathered the staff together to say goodbye.

"Take good care of the place," Frank told the servants. "We'll be back."

Four years later, the Presidential office and the White House were theirs again. And by this time there were three of them, a big Cleveland, a middle-sized Cleveland, and a baby Cleveland.

THE FIRST

The first President to be married while in office was **John Tyler,** in 1844. (Second marriage)

The others were **Grover Cleveland** (first marriage), in 1886, and **Woodrow Wilson** (second marriage), in 1915.

Tidbits & Trivia

EXTRA, EXTRA, READ ALL ABOUT US!

Three newspapermen left the press for the presidential hustings in 1920 when **Warren Harding**, editor of the Marion, Ohio, *Star* took the Republican nomination, **James M. Cox**, owner and publisher of the *Daily News* in Dayton, Ohio, got the nod from the Democrats, and **Robert C. Macauley**, a reporter from the Philadelphia *Inquirer* ran on the Single Tax Party ticket.

CRUELTY TO ANIMALS

William Howard Taft weighed over 300 pounds. Despite exercise, dieting, and outdoor activity, his weight did not drop below this figure. Taft was destined to be a 300-pound man.

Prior to his election as President, he served as Governor General of the Philippines. Because Taft had not been feeling very well, Secretary of War Elihu Root sent the governor a cable asking about his health. Taft cabled back that he was much better, so much better in fact that he had just returned from a 25-mile horseback ride.

Root promptly sent Taft the following cable: "How is the horse?"

THE SMALLEST, HEAVIEST, TALLEST

William Howard Taft
Height, 6 ft.;
weight, 300-340 lbs.

Abraham Lincoln
Height, 6 ft. 4 in.;
weight, 180 lbs.

James Madison
Height, 5 ft. 4 in.;
weight, 100 lbs.

I LIKE THIS JOB BETTER THAN MY OLD JOB

William Howard Taft never had wanted to be President, did not enjoy being President, and was happy when he no longer was President. The only position that he'd ever really wanted in Washington was that of Chief Justice of the Supreme Court.

He finally got it. On June 30, 1921, eight years after his term as President was over, Taft was appointed Chief Justice by Warren Harding and served in the post until 1930. During this period he once commented happily, "In my present life I don't remember that I ever was President."

Taft was the only man ever to occupy the positions of both President and Chief Justice. And he was big enough to do it.

ALL-AMERICAN BOY

James Madison did his country proud when he took the Oath of Office March 4, 1809, for from head to toe he was dressed completely in garments made in the United States.

His "made in America" attire included a Connecticut oxford cloth jacket, breeches woven from the wool of New York sheep, and silk stockings and black shoes manufactured in Massachusetts.

A NOSE FOR PUBLICITY

"Public discussion is helping to doom slavery," remarked **Abraham Lincoln** in 1860.

"What kills a skunk is the publicity it gives itself."

THE PRESIDENTS

THE PRESIDENTS of the UNITED STATES

PRESIDENT	IN OFFICE	PARTY	ZODIAC SIGN
1. George Washington 2/22/1732 - 12/14/1799	4/30/1789 - 3/3/1797	No party [1]	Pisces
2. John Adams 10/30/1735 - 7/4/1826	3/4/1797 - 3/3/1801	Federalist	Scorpio
3. Thomas Jefferson 4/13/1743 - 7/4/1826	3/4/1801 - 3/3/1809	Democratic- Republican	Aries
4. James Madison 3/16/1751 - 6/28/1836	3/4/1809 - 3/3/1817	Democratic- Republican	Pisces
5. James Monroe 4/28/1758 - 7/4/1831	3/4/1817 - 3/3/1825	Democratic- Republican	Taurus
6. John Quincy Adams 7/11/1767 - 2/23/1848	3/4/1825 - 3/3/1829	Democratic- Republican [2]	Cancer
7. Andrew Jackson 3/15/1767 - 6/8/1845	3/4/1829 - 3/3/1837	Democrat	Pisces
8. Martin Van Buren 12/5/1782 - 7/24/1862	3/4/1837 - 3/3/1841	Democrat	Sagittarius
9. William Henry Harrison 2/9/1773 - 4/4/1841	3/4/1841 - 4/4/1841	Whig	Aquarius
10. John Tyler 3/29/1790 - 1/18/1862	4/6/1841 - 3/3/1845	Whig	Aries
11. James Polk 11/2/1795 - 6/15/1849	3/4/1845 - 3/3/1849	Democrat	Scorpio
12. Zachary Taylor 11/24/1784 - 7/9/1850	3/4/1849 - 7/9/1850	Whig	Sagittarius
13. Millard Fillmore 1/7/1800 - 3/8/1874	7/10/1850 - 3/3/1853	Whig	Capricorn
14. Franklin Pierce 11/23/1804 - 10/8/1869	3/4/1853 - 3/3/1857	Democrat	Sagittarius
15. James Buchanan 4/23/1791 - 6/1/1868	3/4/1857 - 3/3/1861	Democrat	Taurus
16. Abraham Lincoln 2/12/1809 - 4/15/1865	3/4/1861 - 4/15/1865	Republican	Aquarius
17. Andrew Johnson 12/29/1808 - 7/31/1875	4/15/1865 - 3/3/1869	National Union [3]	Capricorn
18. Ulysses S. Grant 4/27/1822 - 7/23/1885	3/4/1869 - 3/3/1877	Republican	Taurus
19. Rutherford B. Hayes 10/4/1822 - 1/17/1893	3/4/1877 - 3/3/1881	Republican	Libra

[1] By the end of George Washington's second term he had become closely identified with the Federalists.

[2] John Quincy Adams was a Democratic-Republican but ran as an independent in 1824.

[3] The National Union Party was composed of Republicans and War Democrats. Johnson was a Democrat.

Tidbits & Trivia

THE PRESIDENTS of the UNITED STATES (Continued)

PRESIDENT	IN OFFICE	PARTY	ZODIAC SIGN
20. **James Garfield** 11/19/1831 - 9/19/1881	3/4/1881 - 9/19/1881	Republican	Scorpio
21. **Chester A. Arthur** 10/5/1830 - 11/18/1886	9/20/1881 - 3/3/1885	Republican	Libra
22. **Grover Cleveland** 3/18/1837 - 6/24/1908	3/4/1885 - 3/3/1889	Democrat	Pisces
23. **Benjamin Harrison** 8/20/1833 - 3/13/1901	3/4/1889 - 3/3/1893	Republican	Leo
24. **Grover Cleveland**	3/4/1893 - 3/3/1897		
25. **William McKinley** 1/29/1843 - 9/14/1901	3/4/1897 - 9/14/1901	Republican	Aquarius
26. **Theodore Roosevelt** 10/27/1858 - 1/6/1919	9/14/1901 - 3/3/1909	Republican	Scorpio
27. **William Howard Taft** 9/15/1857 - 3/8/1930	3/4/1909 - 3/3/1913	Republican	Virgo
28. **Woodrow Wilson** 12/28/1856 - 2/3/1924	3/4/1913 - 3/3/1921	Democrat	Capricorn
29. **Warren Harding** 11/2/1865 - 8/2/1923	3/4/1921 - 8/2/1923	Republican	Scorpio
30. **Calvin Coolidge** 7/4/1872 - 1/5/1933	8/3/1923 - 3/3/1929	Republican	Cancer
31. **Herbert Hoover** 8/10/1874 - 10/20/1964	3/4/1929 - 3/3/1933	Republican	Leo
32. **Franklin D. Roosevelt** 1/30/1882 - 4/12/1945	3/4/1933 - 4/12/1945	Democrat	Aquarius
33. **Harry S. Truman** 5/8/1884 - 12/26/1972	4/12/1945 - 1/20/1953	Democrat	Taurus
34. **Dwight D. Eisenhower** 10/14/1890 - 3/28/1969	1/20/1953 - 1/20/1961	Republican	Libra
35. **John F. Kennedy** 5/29/1917 - 11/22/1963	1/20/1961 - 11/22/1963	Democrat	Gemini
36. **Lyndon B. Johnson** 8/27/1908 - 1/22/1973	11/22/1963 - 1/20/1969	Democrat	Virgo
37. **Richard M. Nixon** 1/9/1913 -	1/20/1969 - 8/9/1974	Republican	Capricorn
38. **Gerald R. Ford** 7/14/1913 -	8/9/1974 - 1/20/77	Republican	Cancer
39. **James E. Carter** 10/1/1924 -	1/20/77- 1/20/81	Democrat	Libra
40. **Ronald W. Reagan** 2/6/1911-	1/20/81	Republican	Aquarius

THE PRESIDENTS

EVEN
GEORGE WASHINGTON
HAD A MOTHER

Mary Ball Washington lived long enough to see her son George elected first President of the United States. She did not attend his inauguration. The fact is, Mary Ball Washington seems not really to have approved of George. His activities during the Revolutionary War had made her quite angry. He'd had no right to go off and play general when he should have been home taking care of her.

At considerable personal sacrifice, since he had large holdings but was land-poor, George provided for her financial needs. But it wasn't enough. Not for mother Mary.

She complained to members of the Virginia legislature that she was in desperate need of funds and solicited the official aid of these gentlemen. Upon being told what she had done, George begged her to please stop doing that.

"I am viewed as a delinquent," he wrote to her, "and am considered perhaps by the world as an unjust and undutiful son."

Abraham Lincoln is reported to have said of his mother, "All I am and all I ever hope to be, I owe to her."

It is nowhere recorded that the Father of His Country ever said the same.

JACKASS, INDEED!

Upon receiving a jackass as a gift from the King of Spain, **George Washington** wrote a letter to Lafayette which included the following observation:

"The Jack I have already received from Spain in appearance is fine, but his late royal master, tho' past his grand climacteric, cannot be less moved by female allurements than he is; or when prompted can proceed with more deliberation and majestic solemnity to the matter of procreation."

Tidbits & Trivia

HELEN TAKES A RIDE (OR DID SHE TAKE BILL FOR ONE?)

The first First Lady to ride seated beside her husband for the triumphant inauguration-day carriage ride in the Capital was Helen Taft. **William Taft** thought it was her day, after all: the presidency was her dream, not his. His dream, which was to be chief justice, was not realized until 1921.

At any rate, her presence in the carriage warmed him up, for, as the snow fell, marking the worst blizzard to strike Washington in many years, Taft said, "I always said it would be a cold day when I got to be President of the United States."

SO THERE!

After the inauguration, **William Howard Taft** threw all his 300-plus pounds onto a sofa at the White House, waited for the springs to stop creaking and announced, "I'm President now and I'm tired of being kicked around!"

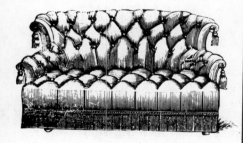

I'LL NEED A MORE GENEROUS OFFER

William Howard Taft was offered a Chair of Law at Yale. He declined it with a twinkle, saying that "a Sofa of Law" was more in keeping with his proportions.

ENERGY CRISIS HITS COUNTRY

"Lights are going out all over the Eastern Seaboard this winter, with Americans bundling up in sweaters and heavy coats, and many of them walking, or taking mass transportation, rather than driving to work.

"Traffic is grinding to a halt, streetlights are dimming, and in New York City alone, 263 pneumonia deaths have been recorded this week. Christmas sales look bleak, restaurants, stores, saloons and auto dealers are losing money.

"Much of the blame is directed at the White House and its chief energy czar, but the President maintains the shortage is real, and not contrived by the energy industry."

Sound familiar? That's no recent news article from the gas-starved seventies, but an energy crisis from another era. The year was 1918, and the President, **Woodrow Wilson**. His energy czar was none other than the son of another President, Dr. Harry A. Garfield, and the nation lacked not gas or oil but another precious form of energy — coal.

THAT WAS QUICK

The 1916 presidential election, **Woodrow Wilson** vs. Charles Evans Hughes, was an extremely close one. As the returns came in, it became evident that the election would be decided by a single state: California. The man who won there would be President.

The first California returns indicated that Hughes was winning. As the trend continued into the evening, certain that he had won, Hughes went to bed. Then the voting tide turned. Wilson caught Hughes, passed him, took California, and won the election.

The next morning, a reporter tried to reach Hughes to tell him what had happened. Before he had a chance to convey the information, the reporter was told brusquely that the President was still asleep and could not be disturbed.

There are such things as golden opportunities, and the reporter then had his. "When he wakes up, give him this message," said the reporter. "Tell him he's no longer President."

THE OTHER PRESIDENT

Jefferson Davis was chosen President of the Confederate States of America by the Provisional Congress of the Confederacy on February 18, 1861. He was not the South's first choice for leadership of the Confederacy: Alexander Stephens, a Georgia Congressman, was offered the presidency initially, but refused because he did not wish "to strike the first blow."

11

THE PRESIDENTS

BUFFALO GAL

In Buffalo, New York, there lived a young widow named Mrs. Maria Halpin. Romantically inclined, Mrs. Halpin had not one but a number of Prince Charmings. Among them was a young bachelor named **Grover Cleveland.**

When a son was born to Mrs. Halpin as a result of her social activities, people wondered just which Prince was the Paternal Prince. It was a highly questionable matter, but Cleveland assumed the responsibility and the support costs, sans marriage.

There were very few who knew about this before Cleveland ran for the presidency. Shortly after the election campaign began, there were very few who didn't.

"What shall we tell the people?" cried Cleveland's managers.

"The truth," said Cleveland, and won.

The campaign provided a little something special for the kids, a bit of doggerel which they ran around repeating for the benefit of voters and doggerel-lovers.

> Ma! Ma!
> Where's my pa?
> Gone to the White House.
> Ha! Ha! Ha!

BETTER THAN NOTHING

In a speech made before the House of Representatives, **James Garfield,** who then occupied a seat for Ohio, told the story of an Englishman who was wrecked on a strange shore. Wandering along the coast, the man came to a gallows with a victim hanging on it. He fell down on his knee and thanked God to see a sign of civilization.

THE LOGIC OF LOVE

Grace Goodhue was a teacher of the deaf when **Calvin Coolidge** proposed to her. Coolidge was well aware of his inclination to taciturnity. "Having taught the deaf to hear," he commented, "she might perhaps teach the mute to speak."

GOOD TRAINING GROUND

As a young man, **Grover Cleveland** was an assistant teacher in an institute for the blind in New York City.

WHITE HOUSE FACTS

Shaking hands with the President at a White House reception was a custom originated by **Thomas Jefferson** at a Fourth of July celebration in 1801. His presidential predecessors, Washington and Adams, had on such occasions bowed.

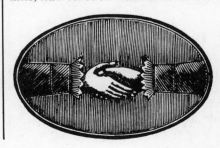

"CAN ANYTHING BE MADE OF THIS?"

Othello
Act III, Scene IV

The winter of 1845-1846 was cold, rainy, and monotonous for the American army stationed at Corpus Christi during the Mexican War.

To help relieve the tedium, the men formed a theatrical group. Among their more ambitious productions was that of Shakespeare's *Othello*.

In this all-soldier production, the part of Desdemona was played by **Ulysses S. Grant.**

SOME GENTLEMEN PREFER BLONDES

Ulysses S. Grant's wife, Julia, was cross-eyed. Julia wanted to have an operation, newly developed at the time, to uncross her eyes. Her husband persuaded her against having the operation. His reason was simple: "I like her that way."

HOW GROVER CLEVELAND LOST TWO VOTES

In 1870, **Grover Cleveland** became sheriff of Erie County, New York. On two occasions Cleveland, in discharging his duties as sheriff, was called upon to serve as official hangman. The man who later became President actually placed and tightened the noose and sprang the trap in the execution of both his job and two convicted murderers.

NUMBER TWO TRIED VERY HARD

The second Mrs. Benjamin Harrison, niece of the first, presented her husband with a daughter on February 21, 1897. The bouncing baby girl was younger than even the youngest of Harrison's four grandchildren, offspring of the children of his first wife.

The first President's child ever born in the White House was Esther Cleveland, the second child of President and Mrs. **Grover Cleveland**, who arrived on September 9, 1893.

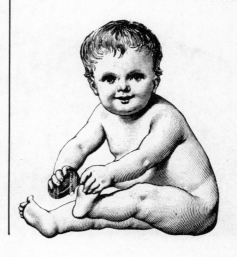

THE PRESIDENTS

I WON'T BE HOME FOR DINNER, I HAVE A MOUNTAIN OF WORK

Mount Rushmore stands in the middle of the Black Hills of South Dakota. It used to be just another faceless 6,000-foot mountain lost in the hills. But then some local residents who were interested in developing the tourist business and a rugged, baldheaded sculptor with a big, bristling moustache and even bigger bristlier ideas got together.

The sculptor's name was John Gutzon Borglum, and he was the kind of fellow to drop the John and keep the Gutzon.

Borglum proposed to carve the stone portraits of major Presidents in the granite east face of the mountain, a 300-foot perpendicular slab 500 feet above the valley below. There would be the faces of four Presidents and he'd pick them.

He wanted to carve **George Washington** for Washington's role in gaining American independence and establishing the Republic.

He wanted to include **Thomas Jefferson** for Jefferson's having made the Louisiana Purchase, which typified the spirit of continental growth.

He wanted the face of **Abraham Lincoln** because Lincoln preserved the Union.

He wanted the image of **Theodore Roosevelt** because he admired the 20th century vigor of that restless all-American President.

The faces are each as high as a five-story building, about 60 feet from chin to top of head. The pupils of the eyes are 4 feet across and the mouths are 18 feet wide.

The carving took 14 years — from 1927 to 1941. No, that's not quite accurate. There were six and a half years spent in carving and seven and a half years in trying to raise the money to keep carving.

The total cost was about $990,000 —over $800,000 from the Federal Government, the rest from private funds. Borglum got $170,000.

And the carving wasn't exactly carving. After Borglum made models, most of the work was done by a crew using pneumatic drills and dynamite. They removed a total of 450,000 tons of stone, and Borglum was proud, as he should have been, that not one of them was killed doing it.

Gutzon Borglum died in 1941, before the work was finished. It was completed by his son, Lincoln. Actually it never was quite finished. Theodore Roosevelt is still a little rough.

Tidbits & Trivia

3 HATS

Following the presidential election of 1880, **James A. Garfield** found himself in a unique position.

He had just been elected to the presidency. Earlier that year he had been elected by the Ohio legislature to serve as a United States Senator from that state, his term to begin the following March.

President-elect, Senator-elect Garfield already had a job. He was, as he had been since 1862, an Ohio member of the U.S. House of Representatives.

JOHN ARMSTRONG... NO RELATION TO JACK

All Presidents have their problems. One of **James Madison's** problems was a man named John Armstrong, Madison's Secretary of War during the War of 1812. At a conference dealing with military conduct of the war, some of those present expressed the fear that the British might attack the city of Washington itself. Since it was in danger, they felt, the national capital should be adequately defended. And what did the Secretary of War have to say?

"Here?" exclaimed Armstrong, "Here to this sheepwalk! Why the devil would they want to come here?"

THE VICE PRESIDENT NOBODY KNEW

Franklin Pierce's Vice President, **William Rufus DeVane King**, may have been the most obscure second banana of all. He didn't even attend the inauguration, and had the oath administered in Cuba instead. He died six weeks later, April 18, 1853, never having presided over the Senate.

ULTERIOR MOTIVE?

James Monroe was a member of a Congressional committee formed to investigate a charge of illegal speculation in government funds against Alexander Hamilton. The investigation, conducted discreetly, established Hamilton's innocence. It seems that James Reynolds, the gentleman bringing the charge, had done so for personal reasons. Hamilton had committed adultery with Mrs. Reynolds. The truth of this was readily admitted by Hamilton but, since adultery was no concern of the government, the investigation was concluded.

A few years later, political enemies of Hamilton found out about the story and published the details in a pamphlet. Hamilton and Monroe were not friends. Assuming that Monroe was in part responsible for the pamphlet — he wasn't — Hamilton challenged Monroe to a duel.

The Monroe-Hamilton duel never took place, but only because cooler heads prevailed, persuading the two men against fighting. The coolest of these cool heads belonged to the man who had agreed to be Monroe's second, Aaron Burr.

PRESIDENTS ON THE PRESIDENCY

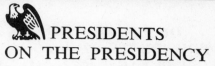

There has never been an hour since I left the White House that I have felt a wish to return to it.

Benjamin Harrison

APPROPRIATE

Martin Van Buren married Hannah Hoes.

Hannah's father was a farmer.

The Farmer Hoes.

THE PRESIDENTS

OCCUPATIONS OF PRESIDENTS—DOCTORS, LAWYERS, BUT NO INDIAN CHIEFS

There are no sure roads to the presidency but if there is one occupation which is more help than hindrance, it is probably law. Twenty-four of the thirty-eight Presidents were admitted to the bar as attorneys, having fulfilled the legal requirements. Not all were graduates of law school; some read for the law under the guidance of an established jurist.

Those who went on to the highest office in the land after hanging up their shingles were: **J. Adams, Jefferson, Monroe, J. Q. Adams, Jackson, Van Buren, Tyler, Polk, Fillmore, Pierce, Buchanan, Lincoln, Hayes, Garfield, Arthur, Cleveland, B. Harrison, McKinley, Taft, Wilson, Coolidge, F. D. Roosevelt, Nixon,** and **Ford. T. Roosevelt** entered law school but then instead he decided for "on the job training" and ran directly for state office. Teddy also moonlighted as an author.

Schoolteaching seems to have helped many keep the wolf from the door before they became President. Seven Presidents were schoolteachers: **J. Adams, Fillmore, Garfield, Arthur, McKinley, Harding** and **L. B. Johnson.** At higher education levels, **Taft** was a law professor, while **Garfield, Wilson** and **Eisenhower** were presidents of colleges or universities.

The military profession can claim four Presidents: **Taylor, Grant, Eisenhower,** and **Carter. Washington** and **W. Harrison** were also good military men but they couldn't wait to get back to farming. **Carter** also can be considered a farmer President but in the vocabulary of today he is listed as having been an agribusinessman.

The other professions which Presidents have pursued prior to holding high office were:

Newspapermen; (three) **Taft, Harding** and **Kennedy**
Surveyors; (three) **Washington, J. Adams** and **Lincoln**
Storekeepers; (two) **Lincoln** and **Truman**
Tailors; (one) **A. Johnson**
Engineers; (one) **Hoover**
Actors; (one) **Reagan**

It is interesting to note that **Madison** is considered the only President whose sole previous occupational experience was—politician.

Tidbits & Trivia

PLENTY OF COLLATERAL, THOUGH

George Washington owned land. He owned land in Virginia, Maryland, Pennsylvania, Kentucky, in the Northwest Territory, and in Washington, D. C.; thousands and thousands of acres in all.

Still, in March of 1789, Washington had to borrow £600 to clean up some debts and to pay for a trip to New York City for his inauguration as President, a ceremony they couldn't very well hold without him.

THE GREAT WASHINGTON'S BIRTHDAY CAPER

George Washington was born February 11, 1731, and every year on that day he grew one year older. That is, until 1751, when his birthday disappeared.

It seems that England, in changing from the Julian to the Gregorian calendar, removed January 1 through March 24 for that year, so that the "short" year ran from March 25 through December 31.

Then an Act of Parliament added eleven days to complete the adjustment, so George celebrated his twentieth birthday on February 22, 1752, by the new calendar two years and eleven days after his nineteenth.

Further adjustments in Washington's birthday continue to confuse. In 1971 President Nixon signed an Executive Order establishing a federal holiday schedule which places Washington's Birthday on the third Monday in February.

IT ALL BEGAN LONG BEFORE GEORGE, EVEN BEFORE THERE WERE ANTACID TABLETS

If you reach back into **George Washington's** English ancestry, the records show direct descent from Laurence Washington, at one time the mayor of Northhampton, who received the grant of a manor in Northhamptonshire from Henry VIII. Further back in time the family name, as might be expected, had variants in spelling — Wasshington, Weschington, Wassington, and in its original form, De Wessyngton.

The Washington line appears to stem from a certain William, noble knight, of the manor and village of Wessyngton. In those times surnames were just beginning to be used, and people often took their last names from the places in which they lived.

Now William De Wessyngton had not always lived in Wessyngton. In 1183 William moved there from another village. That earlier community, still in existence, was known as Hertburn (now Hartburn), and William of Hertburn, roots-grandfather of our first President, is to be thanked for moving his wife, children and chattels to Wessyngton. Otherwise, our Presidents would have as an address 1600 Pennsylvania Avenue, Hertburn D.C., 20500.

THE PRESIDENTS

A LACK OF HARMONY

A musical performance by Miss Margaret Truman was reviewed by Mr. Paul Hume in the *Washington Post*. The review contained the following comments:

"She is flat a good deal of the time . . . cannot sing with anything approaching professional finish . . . communicates almost nothing of the music."

Upon reading the criticism of his daughter's concert, President **Harry S Truman** wrote a note to Mr. Hume. The note contained the following comments:

"I have just read your lousy review buried in the back pages. You sound like a frustrated old man who never made a success, an eight-ulcer man on a four-ulcer job and all four ulcers working.

"I never met you, but if I do you'll need a new nose and a supporter below."

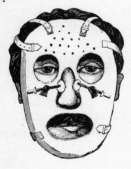

UNPACKED

One wonders how it feels to be relieved of the awesome responsibilities of the presidency. What had ex-President **Harry Truman** done on his first day home again in Independence?

A question like that deserves an answer like that, and Harry provided it:

"I took the suitcases up to the attic."

HOW IT BEGAN

VOICE IN THE CROWD: Give 'em hell, Harry.

HARRY TRUMAN: I never gave 'em hell. I just told the truth and they thought it was hell.

D.D.

GREEKS AND GRANTS

Harry Truman, who as personal emissary of the President along with Lady Bird Johnson attended the funeral of King Paul of Greece in 1964, was irrepressible in spite of the solemnity of the occasion.

"I feel very close to the United States," began Prince Michael, who had welcomed Truman and Mrs. Johnson, "Because my great-great grandfather was aide-de-camp to General Grant."

Slapping the King's cousin on the knee, Truman said, "Well, son, as far as this lady and I are concerned, he was on the wrong side!"

GIVE 'EM HELL, HARRICUM!

When **Harry Truman** received an honorary degree from Oxford in 1956 and a Latin citation addressing him as "Harricum Truman," students in the crowd cheered, "Give 'Em Hell, Harricum!"

LOVE, YOUR MAGIC SPELL IS EVERYWHERE . . . ALMOST

When you're a President's eligible daughter living at the White House, you get to meet a lot of fellows. But from there on, it's uphill all the way. Margaret Truman described the problem.

". . . Consider the effect of saying good night to a boy at the door . . . in a blaze of floodlights, with a Secret Service man in attendance. There is not much you can do but shake hands, and that's no way to get engaged."

HE SAID A NICKEL A POUND AND I SAID I'D NEVER PAY THAT FOR LAMB CHOPS

President **William Henry Harrison,** a market basket on his arm, did the family food shopping.

Tidbits & Trivia

GENERAL WHO?

Clearly unmindful of the First Lady's Southern origins, the Department of the Interior informed Lady Bird Johnson that the first beneficiary of a gift for monument-cleaning in Washington, D.C., would be the statue of General Sherman.

"Does it have to be General Sherman?" she asked. "He's my least-favorite general."

Told that it had to be Sherman, whose statue was the dirtiest and most in need of cleaning, she acquiesced but warned, "Well, let's go ahead and clean him up. But let's just don't announce it."

NOT ME

A lot of people wanted General William Tecumseh Sherman to run for President in 1884. William Tecumseh Sherman was not one of them.

"If nominated, I will not accept," he said. "If elected, I will not serve."

He also said, "If forced to choose between the penitentiary and the White House for four years, I would say the penitentiary, thank you."

ALL WOOL AND A YARD WIDE

During World War I, the **Woodrow Wilsons** did what every homeowner dreams about. In order to release White House groundskeepers for the war effort, they kept a herd of sheep on the White House lawn to eat the grass.

Not only did the grass remain short, but eating it provided the sheep with very heavy coats of wool. The sheep were shorn and the wool was sold, providing nearly $100,000 to the Red Cross, a lot more than they would have made using groundskeepers.

PLAN AHEAD

An observation on President **William McKinley** by William Allen White:

"He was destined for a statue in the park and he was practicing the pose for it."

A KING FOR PRESIDENT

Once upon a time there was a King who became President of the United States.

When he was still very young, his parents were divorced and he was adopted by his stepfather and given a new name. Instead of Leslie King, Jr., he became **Gerald Ford, Jr.**

And may he and we live happily ever after.

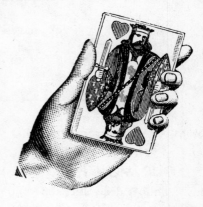

"FATHER'S DAY"

Gerald Ford, whose natural father deserted him and his mother, never forgot the hardship he and others all over the country had faced under similar circumstances. The first day of every new Congress, he introduced what was known as the "Runaway Pappy Bill," legislation which would require the government to help wives find the men who had deserted their children so that the wives could claim support money. Ford felt that Uncle Sam, who had all the security records, should lend a hand in finding those "dear old dads."

THE PRESIDENTS

IF YOU'RE GONNA SHOOT OFF YOUR MOUTH . . .

They called **Andrew Jackson** "Old Hickory." Hickory is tough. So was Andy. He was no man to insult, especially at a time when dueling was considered a more satisfactory way to answer an insult than a lot of name-calling. Charlie Dickinson found that out.

Charlie made a nasty remark about Mrs. Jackson. Rachel Jackson was a divorcee when she married Andy. Or rather thought she was. Technically her divorce wasn't final until some time after the Jacksons were married. They had a second ceremony, but in the meantime they had committed adultery, and Andy didn't like to be reminded about it. Charlie Dickinson reminded him. Andy replied by challenging Dickinson to a duel with pistols.

The duel took place at Harrison's Mills, Kentucky, on May 30, 1806. Charlie fired first, and his bullet

hit Andy in the chest. Then Andy fired. Charlie went down. That night he died.

The bullet in Andy's chest was too close to his heart to be removed safely, so he carried it for the rest of his life. Since the whole matter had concerned an affair of the heart, this was somehow appropriate.

SOLDIERS OF FORTUNE AND FORTUNATE SOLDIERS

Some of our chief executives were war heroes; **Washington, Jackson, Grant** and **Eisenhower** were famous generals, and others like **Kennedy, Ford, Nixon, Johnson** and **Reagan** served their country in uniform during wartime.

But the call to duty has not always been sweet — Washington himself resigned his commission at 26, despairing of further advancement after fighting the French and Indian War, and Grant resigned barely ten years out of West Point. Nor has duty's call always been answered. In the case of **Grover Cleveland,** "drafted" into the Union Army during the Civil War, he declined the honor, paid a substitute $150 to serve in his place, and stayed home to support his mother and sister while his two other brothers were off fighting for the Union. Cleveland's actions were completely legal under the terms of the Conscription Act of 1863.

HOW WAS THAT AGAIN?

Never known as our most intellectual President, **Grover Cleveland** seems to have learned a few things, particularly where vocabulary was concerned. When Congress asked him to produce certain documents and papers under a little-used statute passed twenty years earlier, he sputtered, "innocuous desuetude," and won his case.

All of which shows the power of a few well-chosen words on the subject of "benign neglect."

Tidbits & Trivia

ANCHORS AWEIGH, FINALLY

For 172 years, from the very beginning, the presidency was occupied either by men who had served in the Army or men who had seen no military service at all. There was not a Navy man among them.

In 1960 all that changed. Once it did, it was a 180° turn and full speed ahead:

John Kennedy — Navy, **Lyndon Johnson** — Navy, **Richard Nixon** — Navy, **Gerald Ford** — Navy, **James Carter** — Navy.

Five in a row for the Navy.

HE'S ENTITLED

There were Joseph Kennedy and his wife, Rose Fitzgerald Kennedy.

There were the children: Joe, Jr., John (Jack), Rosemary, Kathleen, Eunice, Patricia, Robert, and Jean.

There was a family sailboat. It was called *Tenofus*.

Then, along came Edward, and they needed a bigger sailboat.

The name of the new sailboat was *Onemore*.

When Father spoke, everyone in the Kennedy family listened, even if one happened to be the newly elected President of the United States.

The day was pleasant, and Joe Kennedy decided it would be nice if they all went sailing. Jack didn't feel like going and said so. This simply wasn't done. They all looked at Jack. Then they all looked at Father. Joseph Kennedy was silent for a moment. Then he said,

"I don't think the President should have to go if he doesn't want to."

THE FIRST

The first President to cross the Atlantic was **Woodrow Wilson,** aboard the S.S. *George Washington,* shortly after the end of World War I, in December 1918.

IN THE FLESH

William Howard Taft took the honors for presidential girth, but **Grover Cleveland,** weighing in at about 260, was Number 2. He was called, among other things, Uncle Jumbo.

On a presidential campaign trip, Cleveland's train stopped at a small town where a crowd had gathered to see the President. A grizzled old man made his way through the crowd, pushed up close to Cleveland, and stared at him.

"So you're the President," the man said to Cleveland.

"I am," said Cleveland.

"I've voted for a good many Presidents," said the man, "but you're the first one I ever saw."

Cleveland smiled. "Well, what do you think?"

The old man looked at Cleveland admiringly. "You're a whopper," he said.

THE PRESIDENTS

A DIFFERENT MEASURE OF THE MAN

What the Presidents were worth when they died, keeping in mind that:

A. There is no information on certain presidents who considered it their own damn business (see last column).

B. A dollar is no longer worth it.

C. This is simply for the pleasure of curious readers and is not to be used for accounting purposes.

WHEN THE CHEERING, AND THE INCOME, STOPPED

Many former Presidents, having dipped deep into personal fortunes during their administrations, retired heavily in debt. Some of their widows were actually poverty-stricken.

Yet it wasn't until 1958 that government pensions were provided for them. In fact, President Truman's comment to House Speaker Sam Rayburn that he needed federal help to "keep ahead of the hounds," may have hastened the passage of the Former Presidents Act.

It seems, however, that as far as ex-Presidents went, the Congress thought genteel poverty may have been perfectly in order, for a Senate Committee noted in considering a stipend for ex-Presidents that, "We expect a former President to engage in no business or occupation which would demean the office he has held or capitalize upon in any improper way. There are many ways in which a former President can earn a large income, but ought not to."

Broke

Jefferson
Monroe
William Harrison
Grant (made $500,000 posthumously from his memoirs on the Civil War)

$25,000-100,000

John Adams
John Quincy Adams
Pierce
Lincoln
Andrew Johnson

$100,000-500,000

Polk
Taylor
Cleveland
Benjamin Harrison
McKinley
Taft
Harding

$500,000-1,000,000

Washington
Theodore Roosevelt
Wilson
Coolidge
Truman
Eisenhower

Over $1,000,000

Hoover
Franklin Roosevelt
Kennedy
Lyndon Johnson

Estate not known

Madison
Jackson
Van Buren
Tyler
Fillmore
Buchanan
Hayes
Garfield
Arthur

Tidbits & Trivia

IT DOES HAVE ITS COMPENSATIONS

Benjamin Franklin thought the President should receive no salary at all. He made that proposal to the Constitutional Convention in 1787, stating as his reasons:

"There are two passions which have a powerful influence on the affairs of men. These are ambition and avarice, the love of power and the love of money. Separately, each of these has great force in prompting men to action, but when united in view of the same object, they have in many minds the most violent effects . . ."

The good Doctor Franklin was listened to respectfully and his proposal ignored. Terms of presidential compensation were agreed upon. Through the years, these have changed. Here are the salaries and fringe benefits which Presidents have received.

PRESIDENTIAL SALARIES (YEARLY BASIS)

$25,000 salary
> **George Washington — Ulysses S. Grant** (first term)

$50,000 salary
> **Ulysses S. Grant** (second term) — **Theodore Roosevelt**

$75,000 salary (taxable)
+ $25,000 travel allowance (non taxable)
> **William H. Taft — Franklin Roosevelt**

$100,000 salary (taxable)
+ $40,000 travel and entertainment allowance (non taxable)
+ $50,000 expense account (taxable)
> **Harry Truman — Lyndon Johnson**

$200,000 salary (taxable)
+ $40,000 travel and entertainment allowance (non taxable)
+ $50,000 expense account (taxable)
> **Richard Nixon — Ronald Reagan**

RETIREMENT BENEFITS

Annual pension — $60,000
Office and staff expenses — $96,000
Civil Service retirement benefits — up to $18,000/yr.
Free office space
Free mailing privileges
Free use of government planes
Secret Service protection
Widow's annual pension — $20,000

HELP WANTED

Four-year position available (may be renewed); must be over 35 yrs of age, & a U.S. resident 14 yrs; no foreigners need apply: natural-born citizens only will be considered. Salary, $200,000; housing included, also weekend camp; free travel, other fringe benefits. Fondness for dogs and people helpful. Good opportunity for right person; ample pension. Warning: this job may be dangerous to your health.

THE PRESIDENTS

WHERE WAS THE ASSISTANT SECRETARY OF THE NAVY?

Newly sworn in as **Wilson's** Assistant Secretary of the Navy, **FDR** wrote his mother:

"I am baptized, confirmed, sworn in, vaccinated — and somewhat at sea!!!"

ONLY JOKING ???

Prior to the 1924 campaign, **FDR** received a note from his former boss, Secretary of the Navy Josephus Daniels, who kidded him:

"I think the *World* showed good taste when it announced that you were taking the helm of the Smith campaign, they published the picture of your wife. I have had that experience on similar occasions and have always wondered how the newspapermen knew so well who was at the head of the family."

Franklin replied lightly:

"You are right about the squaws! Like you I have fought for years to keep my name on the front page and to relegate the wife's to the advertising section. My new plan, however, seems admirable— hereafter for three years my name will not appear at all, but each fourth year (presidential one) I am to have all the limelight."

THE FOURTH ESTATE

President **F. D. Roosevelt** once handed a reporter the Nazi Iron Cross when he was asked an impertinent question. He also regularly told offending scribes to "put on dunce cap" or "go stand in a corner."

Harry Truman called columnist Drew Pearson an SOB, but said, "When the press stops abusing me, I'll know I'm in the wrong pew."

Woodrow Wilson was the first to hold regular White House press conferences, but the idea didn't catch on, although **Harding** revived it briefly; **Coolidge** and **Hoover** would answer reporters' questions only in writing, and with reluctance.

Ike initiated the taped TV news conference, but **Kennedy** relished live ones. He said it put him "In the bull's-eye!"

FDR holds the news conference record, 998 of them in 12 years in office. **Truman** averaged 40 per year, **Ike** 24, **Kennedy** 21 and **Johnson** 25.

SAY CHEESE

The engineer on **FDR's** 1920 campaign train proved prophetic, even though Franklin lost his bid for the vice-presidency: "That lad's got a 'million vote smile,'" the trainman said, "and mine's going to be one of them."

FOOD FADS

The New Frontier was defined by **Jack Kennedy's** cole slaw, and **Lyndon Johnson** got fired up for the War on Poverty by eating chili. **Dick Nixon** was known to order up cottage cheese and ketchup. **Jimmy Carter** did almost as much for peanuts as George Washington Carver. Now, **Ronald Reagan** dispenses jelly beans at cabinet meetings. But when the old movies are being run off after hours, Ronnie reveals his true colors as a popcorn freak.

Tidbits & Trivia

WHAT THIS COUNTRY NEEDED WASN'T HIM

Woodrow Wilson's Vice-President, **Thomas Riley Marshall**, might have succeeded to the presidency when Wilson suffered his stroke had not Wilson himself, his wife, doctors and advisors all agreed it would be a disaster if the Vice-President took over. Marshall routinely refused to go to cabinet meetings and avoided any and all responsibility, commenting that if he couldn't have the $75,000 that went with the President's job, he wouldn't do any of the work.

His greatest accomplishment was to coin the phrase, "What this country needs is a good 5¢ cigar."

A VOTE OF NO CONFIDENCE

Woodrow Wilson, paying a duty call on a very old and very deaf aunt, was dismayed that the lady hadn't kept up with his progress.

"How are you employed these days?" she asked.

"I've been elected President," he answered.

"Of what?" she inquired.

"Of the United States," he told her proudly.

"Don't be silly," she retorted, and put her ear trumpet away in disgust.

LADY BIRD AND THE PORTRAIT OF DORIAN GRAY

Mrs. Johnson once admitted that every time she passed the portrait of **Woodrow Wilson** which hung in the Red Room, she saw "what a toll the presidency takes on a man."

DR. PRESIDENT

Woodrow Wilson was the only Chief Executive to have earned his Ph.D.

"LET ME COUNT THE WAYS"

During their 29-year marriage, **Woodrow Wilson** and his first wife, Ellen, exchanged some 1,400 love notes, writing them to each other whenever they were separated.

That's about 1,400 more love notes than a lot of couples ever exchange.

EITHER WAY, HE WINS

The beautiful widow had at first told **Woodrow Wilson** she would marry him only if he were defeated in his bid for reelection.

The articulate Wilson, however, finally persuaded her to change her mind, and Edith Bolling Galt became Mrs. Woodrow Wilson December 18, 1915. Next morning, the Secret Service observed the bridegroom in his cutaway prancing down the aisle of the honeymoon train whistling, "Oh, you beautiful doll!"

He also won the election.

PITHY FROM WOODY

Woodrow Wilson said it. "Conservatism is the policy of 'make no change and consult your grandmother when in doubt.'"

THE PRESIDENTS

CHANGE GOALS

Jimmy Carter had not always aspired to the presidency. At one time, his ambitions were somewhat more modest.

"When I was a midshipman at Annapolis," he acknowleges, "the only thing I wanted to be was Chief of Naval Operations."

ONLY ONE...

Only one President had a PhD. **Woodrow Wilson** received his doctorate from Johns Hopkins University in 1886. The subject of his doctoral thesis was "Congressional Government, a Study in American Politics."

He learned more about this subject later.

SOME U.S. PRESIDENTS ALSO WERE U. PRESIDENTS

Presidents **Garfield, Wilson,** and **Eisenhower** also served as presidents of institutions of higher learning. Garfield was president of Hiram College, Wilson of Princeton University, and Eisenhower of Columbia University.

George Washington and **John Tyler** both were chancellors of William and Mary, and **Millard Fillmore** chancellor of the University of Buffalo.

SON OF HARVARD TURNS CRIMSON

When Harvard University conferred an honorary degree upon President **Andrew Jackson** in 1833, it was understandable that Jackson's losing presidential opponent and Harvard alumnus, **John Quincy Adams,** was outraged.

Dashing off an indignant note to authorities at the University, Adams seethed: "As myself an affectionate child of our alma mater, I would not be present to witness her disgrace in conferring her highest literary honors upon a barbarian who could not write a sentence of grammar and hardly could spell his own name."

SUMMER EMPLOYMENT

During two summer vacations while he was in high school, **Richard Nixon** worked in Prescott, Arizona, as a barker for the wheel of chance at the "Slippery Gulch Rodeo."

ACADEMICALLY INCLINED

Three Presidents were elected to Phi Beta Kappa for their academic performance as college undergraduates: **John Quincy Adams,** Bachelor of Arts, Harvard College, Class of 1787; **Chester A. Arthur,** Bachelor of Arts, Union College, Class of 1848; **Theodore Roosevelt,** Bachelor of Arts, Harvard University, Class of 1880.

WELL-SCHOOLED

He was a mule driver and a bargeman on the Erie Canal, a professor of Latin and Greek, later president at Hiram College, Ohio, an army general, a member of the House of Representatives, and President of the United States. These were steps in the many-faceted life of **James Garfield.**

Garfield was a graduate of Williams, and attended the school when Mark Hopkins, noted 19th-century educator, was its president. His association with Hopkins prompted Garfield to make a remark which can be well-appreciated by anyone paying the bills for today's higher and higher and higher education tuition costs.

"My idea of the ideal college," he said, "is a log, with a student at one end of it and Mark Hopkins at the other."

A MAN MUST DO WHAT HE MUST DO

William Henry Harrison wished to be a doctor, and for several months he studied medicine at the University of Pennsylvania.

Apparently the saving of human lives was not for him. In a somewhat abrupt career about-face, he withdrew from medical school and became a professional soldier.

Tidbits & Trivia

PRESIDENTIAL SCHOOL DAYS

College Graduates	College
J. Adams	Harvard
J. Q. Adams	Harvard
T. Roosevelt	Harvard
F. Roosevelt	Harvard
Kennedy	Harvard
Jefferson	William and Mary
Tyler	William and Mary
Madison	Princeton
Wilson	Princeton
Grant	West Point
Eisenhower	West Point
Polk	North Carolina
Pierce	Bowdoin
Buchanan	Dickinson
Hayes	Kenyon
Garfield	Williams
Arthur	Union
B. Harrison	Miami (Ohio)
Taft	Yale
Harding	Ohio Central
Coolidge	Amherst
Hoover	Stanford
L. Johnson	Southwest Texas State
Nixon	Whittier
Ford	Michigan
Carter	Annapolis
Reagan	Eureka

Graduated from Law School	Law School
Hayes	Harvard
Taft	Cincinnati
Wilson	Virginia
Nixon	Duke
Ford	Yale

Attended but didn't graduate	College Attended
Monroe	William and Mary
W. H. Harrison	Hampden-Sydney
McKinley	Allegheny

Didn't go to College

Washington
Jackson
Van Buren
Taylor
Fillmore
Lincoln
A. Johnson
Cleveland
Truman

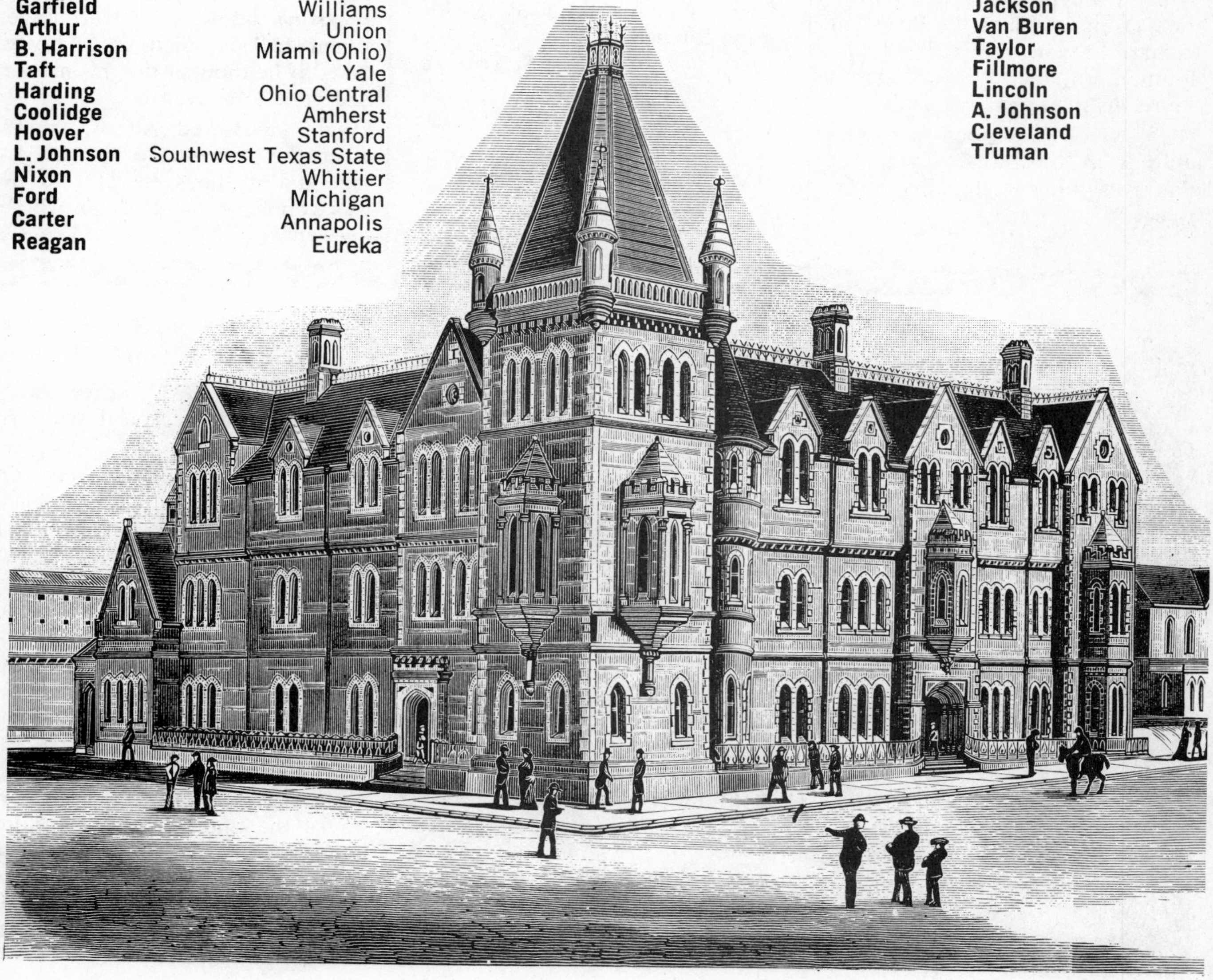

THE PRESIDENTS

YOU PLAY IT YOUR WAY, I'LL PLAY IT MINE

Upon presenting a Steinway piano to ex-President **Harry Truman** at the Truman Library, President **Richard Nixon** referred to Mr. Truman as the White House's "most distinguished pianist."

Then Nixon described his own abilities in this area, saying, "I play everything in the Key of G, by ear."

PRESIDENTS ON THE PRESIDENCY

Being a President is like riding a tiger. A man has to keep riding or be swallowed.

* * *

This administration is going to be cussed and discussed for years to come.

* * *

The buck stops here.

* * *

If you don't like the heat, get out of the kitchen.

Harry S. Truman

IF THAT'S WHAT HE SAID, THAT'S WHAT HE DID

Alfred was a retainer at **Andrew Jackson's** home, The Hermitage. When Jackson died, Alfred was asked if he thought that his master had gone to heaven.

"Well," answered Alfred, "that's where he always said he was going, and if the General said he was gonna go there, that's where he went."

THINGS HAVEN'T CHANGED MUCH

Way back in 1823 **Andrew Jackson** criticized the social scene in Washington:

"There is nothing done here but vissiting (sic) and carding each other — you know how much I was disgusted with those scenes when you and I were here, it has been increased instead of diminishing."

Almost a century later, in 1913, Eleanor Roosevelt, then the Assistant Secretary of the Navy's wife, said, "I've paid 60 calls in Washington this week and been to a luncheon at the Marine barracks, the kind, where the curtains are drawn & candles lit & course after course reduces you to a state of coma which makes it almost impossible to struggle to your feet & leave at 4 P.M."

Tidbits & Trivia

SLOWLY THE CABINET OPENS...

On January 13, 1966, **Lyndon Johnson** appointed Robert C. Weaver to the position of Secretary of Housing and Urban Development.

Weaver was the first black ever appointed to the cabinet by a President from below the Mason-Dixon Line. Or above the Mason-Dixon Line.

HE NEVER MADE SENATOR

The Lincoln-Douglas debates thrust **Abraham Lincoln** into national prominence. Somewhat obscured by the importance of the debates — their clarification of the slavery question — was a more local matter. The men were stating their respective positions in order to win a Senate seat from Illinois.

Lincoln won national prominence, but Douglas won the seat.

The loss occasioned Lincoln to say that he felt like the boy who had stubbed his toe. It hurt too bad to laugh and he was too big to cry.

BETSY ROSS, YOU DIDN'T FINISH THE JOB

Before 1916 there was no official President's flag. There had been a few amateur emblems about from time to time, but it was not until **Woodrow Wilson's** administration that the presidential act got classy. Executive Order No. 2,390, dated May 29, 1916, called for the Presidential seal and four white stars on a blue field. In 1945 **Harry Truman** made several minor changes and increased the number of stars to forty-eight, one for each state. In 1959 **Eisenhower** added the forty-ninth and fiftieth stars.

NOT CRAMPED

Homey it wasn't. As **Thomas Jefferson** described it, the White House was "a great stone house, big enough for two emperors, one Pope, and the Grand Lama into the bargain."

WILL THE REAL MR. HOOVER PLEASE STAND UP?

When **Herbert Hoover** moved into the White House, a monumental problem came to light in that the Executive Mansion's chief usher, Ike Hoover, had the same name. Clearly, there could not be two "Mister Hoovers" in the White House.

Although Ike had been there since the administration of Benjamin Harrison, the problem was solved with Ike taking the name of "Mister Usher."

FAMILY TRADITION

A dinner for White House correspondents in the spring of 1945 was attended by **Franklin Roosevelt,** recently elected to his fourth term as President. Master of Ceremonies was Bob Hope, who drew a loud laugh from his audience, especially from FDR, when he said, "I've always voted for Franklin Roosevelt for President. My father before me always voted for Franklin Roosevelt for President."

THE PRESIDENTS

LET'S START WITH THAT

In 1797, **John Quincy Adams** was appointed United States Minister to Prussia.

After a difficult journey, the newly-married Adams and his bride arrived at the city of Berlin. They were stopped at the gates by a young Prussian army officer. Adams presented his credentials to the officer and explained that he was from the United States. The explanation was apparently insufficient. The officer looked at Adams suspiciously.

"The United States? What are they?" he asked.

CHILDISH ARGUMENT

In his diary of April 25, 1771, **John Adams** recorded the following story which he'd heard the previous day while dining with friends. The story concerned the "Answer of a Young Fellow to the Father of a Girl."

"The Father caught the young Fellow naked in Bed with his Daughter. The old man broke out into reproaches.

'You wretch. What do you mean by trying to get my Daughter with Child?'

'I try to get your Daughter with Child?' the young Fellow protested. 'Oh, No. I was trying Not to get her with Child.'"

JQA AND THE EDUCATION OF HENRY ADAMS

In his autobiography, *The Education of Henry Adams,* the author recalls a day when, as a six- or seven-year-old, he was on an extended visit to the home of his grandfather, **John Quincy Adams.** "He distinctly remembered standing at the house door one summer morning in a passionate outburst of rebellion against going to school . . .

"Henry showed a certain tactical ability by refusing to start, and he met all efforts at compulsion by successful, though too vehement protest. He was in fair way to win, and was holding his own, . . . [when] the door of the President's library opened, and the old man slowly came out. Putting on his hat, he took the boy's hand without a word, and walked with him . . . up the road to the town. After the first moments of consternation . . . the boy reflected that an old gentleman close on eighty would never trouble himself to walk a mile on a hot summer morning over a shadeless road to take a boy to school, and that it would be strange if a lad imbued with the passion of freedom could not find a corner to dodge around, somewhere before reaching the school door . . .

"But the old man did not stop, and the boy saw all his strategical points turned, one after another, until he found himself seated inside the school, and obviously the centre of curious if not malevolent criticism. Not till then did the President release his hand and depart."

Tidbits & Trivia

THE BARE FACTS

John Quincy Adams was a skinny-dipper. Not just a casual skinny-dipper, a regular. Every day, weather permitting, he would rise, walk down to the Potomac River, hang his clothes on a tree, and skinnydip there.

Mrs. Anne Royall was a reporter. To describe her as a "common scold" might seem unkind. However, credence was given to that description in the highly unprejudiced setting of a court of law. Mrs. Royall was once arrested, tried, and convicted of the charge of being a "common scold," and sentenced to the ducking stool.

When Mrs. Royall wished to obtain an exclusive interview with President Adams, it was a simple matter. Being Mrs. Royall and a good reporter as well, she simply followed some of the basic rules of journalism: Who, What, When, and Where.

History has it that her interview with the President went swimmingly.

TO EACH HIS OWN

President **Kennedy** had many a pool party at the White House, where coed swimming in the nude was reported to be the rule, rather than the exception.

Nixon put an end to the skinny-dipping and had the pool converted into office space.

The pool was back again during the **Ford** administration, but swimming was strictly a "suits-on" affair.

THANKS, GEORGE

In October 1789 **George Washington** proclaimed Thursday, November 26, of that year as the first national Thanksgiving.

THE FIRST

The first President to live in the White House was **John Adams,** who moved in on November 1, 1800. He occupied the Executive Mansion for only four months, having lived during most of his term at Philadelphia.

The day after his arrival, Adams wrote to his wife, who had remained in Philadelphia, "I pray heaven to bestow the best of blessings on this house and all that shall hereafter inhabit it. May none but wise and honest men ever rule under this roof."

JACKIE ON JACKIE

When Jacqueline Kennedy told a close friend she was going to marry Aristotle Onassis, her confidant said, "But, Jackie, you're going to fall off your pedestal."

Jackie replied, "That's better than freezing there."

THE PRESIDENTS

BIG MAN ON CAMPUS

At Whittier College, Chairman of the Annual Bonfire was an honored position. For days, students would scour the neighborhood of the campus gathering scrap wood and putting it on the pile in anticipation of a spectacular blaze.

The Bonfire Chairman was in charge of this activity, but he had another unique and important responsibility. It was his job to obtain, by whatever means were necessary (and no questions asked), an outhouse to place on top of the pyre. Some chairmen were unable to meet the challenge, and those years the fire burned without privy.

A chairman who obtained a one-holer had done his job well. A chairman who provided a two-holer had done his job superbly well.

When **Richard Nixon** was Chairman of the Annual Bonfire at Whittier College, topping the pile, to the wonderment of all, was a four-holer.

BEST SEAT IN THE HOUSE

Rumor says that **Gerald Ford** received a toilet seat with the seal of the University of Michigan, his alma mater, proudly displayed. He liked it so well he had it installed in the White House.

MOST POWERFUL FIRST LADY?

When Rosalyn Carter was asked, before her husband's election, what he had that **Gerald Ford** did not, she replied, "he has me."

That should have been a clue to her relationship with the President, for she soon emerged as the most influential and powerful First Lady in memory.

"I have an awesome responsibility and many opportunities as First Lady," she said. "I seek advice and I get it. I am never turned down. The President of the United States cares what I think. I find myself in the eye of history. I have influence, and I know it!"

Observers agree she is appropriately nicknamed "The Steel Magnolia."

JOHN'S FRIEND

John Tyler wrote the following inscription, which appears on the grave of his horse:

"Here lies the body of my good horse, 'The General'. For twenty years he bore me around the circuit of my practice, and in all that time he never made a blunder. Would that his master could say the same."

DISHES TELL THE TALE

The White House Curator, Clement Conger, may have known before anyone that President **Nixon** was going to resign. A week or so before the event, Pat Nixon called him to cancel the order for the Nixon china, for which a preliminary design in cobalt blue and white had been sketched.

"I won't explain, Clem, but don't go ahead with the porcelain. Call it off," Mrs. Nixon said.

"Her voice was quivering. I knew what she meant," Conger recalled. "We stopped work on everything."

CHIPPING IN

The problem of restocking White House china cabinets was not resolved by the less-than-imperial Presidents after Nixon. Both Ford and Carter got by with the old china of earlier administrations. After **Ronald Reagan** took over the lease, Nancy Reagan ordered 220 place settings in red and gold Lenox china at a cost of $209,508.

To keep the household budget from getting out of hand, the bill for the new dinner service was paid for by private donations.

Tidbits & Trivia

THAT WAS NO LADY

In spite of every precaution, White House savoir faire sometimes leaves a great deal to be desired.

When Queen Elizabeth visited during **Gerald Ford's** administration and the President swung her on to the dance floor, the orchestra played, "The Lady is a Tramp."

WORST COOK

Eleanor Roosevelt cheerfully admitted she was a terrible cook, but could whip up great scrambled eggs for Sunday night supper. When the King of England came to dinner, she served hot dogs.

BODY LANGUAGE

Upon being informed that her husband, Franklin, had been nominated by the Democratic Party to run for the presidency in 1852, Mrs. Jane Pierce fainted.

EDITH ON ELEANOR

First Lady Edith Roosevelt, wife of **Theodore Roosevelt**, was fond of her husband's shy, awkward niece, Eleanor, who herself later became First Lady.

"Poor little thing," Edith said. "She is very plain. Her mouth and teeth seem to have no future. But the ugly duckling may turn out to be a swan."

MA GIVES HARRY HELL

Harry Truman's mother never forgave President Lincoln or the U.S. Government for incarcerating her and her Confederate family in a federal camp during the Civil War, and she never let Harry forget it. When she visited Harry in the White House, she told him she'd rather sleep on the floor than in the Lincoln bed, and, what's more, she didn't want her son showing any affection for Old Abe, either.

When, at 92, she broke her hip and Harry flew to her bedside, she snapped, "I don't want any smart cracks out of you. I saw your picture in the paper last week putting a wreath at the Lincoln Memorial."

CAL IS "GRACEFUL"

"Silent" **Cal Coolidge** was remarkably chatty when embarked on the subject of his wife Grace and their courtship. Speaking at length for once, he explained:

"We became engaged in the early summer of 1905 and were married at her home in Burlington, Vermont, on October 4 of that year. I have seen so much fiction on the subject that I may be pardoned for relating the plain facts. We thought we were made for each other.

"For about a quarter of a century she has borne with my infirmities, and I have rejoiced in her graces."

HOW CAL KEPT ON TOP OF THINGS

Every so often, **Calvin Coolidge** would press all the buttons on the President's desk, hide behind a door in his office, and watch secretaries, aides, military men and members of his staff rush in. When the Secret Service arrived with guns drawn, Cal popped out from behind the door and said, "Just wanted to see if everyone's working."

THE PRESIDENTS

PARTY MAN

There were no invitations issued to **Andrew Jackson's** inaugural reception held at the White House on March 4, 1829.

Dress was informal and there was no planned entertainment. Guests were expected to amuse themselves, and they did. Activities at the affair included:

Breaking china, breaking crystal, breaking glasses, breaking windows, standing on damask chairs with muddy boots, destroying so-fas, pulling down wall hangings, tearing clothes, fainting, fighting, getting drunk, and crushing each other.

Described by one of the more literary of the party-goers as a "Saturnalia," the festivities left few unscathed. Fortunately, one of these was President Jackson, but only because a cordon of his stronger friends surrounded him, which prevented his being crushed, and permitted him to escape through a rear window.

Jackson spent his first presidential night at a hotel.

That did it, you say? Never again? Wrong!

Shortly before Jackson left office, the New York State dairymen presented a gift to the outgoing President. The present was a cheese. Not just a cheese. A 4-foot long, 2-foot thick cheese that weighed 1,400 pounds.

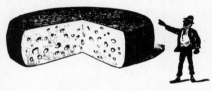

Well, he couldn't possibly eat all that cheese by himself, now could he? There was only one thing to do. Have another party.

The principal difference between the inaugural party and the farewell party was the smell. Uneaten cheese trodden into carpets and smeared on furniture can smell. It can smell for weeks, especially the residue of a 4-foot long and 2-foot thick 1,400-pound cheese.

Long after the party was over, the memory lingered on.

MADISON AND MONROE, INC., A VERY SMALL BUSINESS VENTURE

James Madison and **James Monroe** decided to become partners in a land speculation operation that would, they felt sure, make them rich. Land in the Mohawk Valley looked good to them, and after checking with their land expert, **George Washington,** the two friends contracted for 1,000 acres at $1.50 an acre.

They ran into a problem immediately: the $700 down payment. Madison had no money. Fortu-

nately, Monroe had a little, so he took care of the down payment. One year later, the balance became due. This time neither one of them had any money. The note was extended for three years.

By this time, Madison had some money but Monroe didn't. Madison bought out Monroe, held on to the land for a few years, and finally sold it at a modest profit for a deal of that kind. The investment had hardly provided great wealth.

As businessmen, the partners proved to be excellent Presidents.

Tidbits & Trivia

STAY-AT-HOME SALLY

Sarah Polk outlived her husband by 42 years. In all that time she never again left her home, except to go to church.

HERE'S NOT LOOKING AT YOU

There are no known pictures of two Presidents' wives: Martha Jefferson and Margaret Taylor. Biographers have "guessed" what they might look like by artists' renderings based on pictures of their daughters, whom they were said to resemble.

ROCKY ROAD TO ROMANCE

Lou Henry loved the study of geology and was fascinated with the subject of the "bones of the earth." She went to Stanford University to study and, after class one day, discussed a certain rock with the professor and another student.

The professor asked the young man if the specimen was, as Miss Henry suggested, precarboniferous, or carboniferous instead. **Herbert Hoover** declined to comment, finding the girl more interesting than the stone.

NOT TOO ACCURATE AS PREDICTIONS GO

On November 6, 1962, after being defeated in the California gubernatorial election, future President **Richard Nixon** announced to reporters, "You won't have Nixon to kick around any more, because, Gentlemen, this is my last press conference."

FIGURE OF SPEECH

Lyndon Johnson claimed that there are, essentially, two kinds of speeches.

The first is the Mother Hubbard speech which covers everything but touches nothing.

The second is the Bikini speech, which covers only the essential points.

PRESIDENTS ON THE PRESIDENCY

A few hair shirts are part of the wardrobe of every man. The President differs from other men in that he has a more extensive wardrobe.

Herbert Hoover

THE PRESIDENTS

 **CAPRICORN**
December 22
January 19

Ambitious. Rigid and reserved. Extreme likes and dislikes. Conservative. Not easily swayed. A fighter. Highly industrious.

Presidents born under Capricorn: **Fillmore, A. Johnson, Wilson, Nixon**

 **ARIES**
March 21
April 19

Energetic. Bold in emergency. Self-reliant. Intellectual. Welcomes a challenge. Likes the limelight. Enthusiastic.

Presidents born under Aries: **Jefferson, Tyler**

 **AQUARIUS**
January 20
February 18

Deep understanding and feeling for humanity. A strong faith. Philosophical. Tolerant. Not afraid of commitment. Magnetic.

Presidents born under Aquarius: **W. H. Harrison, Lincoln, McKinley, F.D. Roosevelt, Reagan**

 **TAURUS**
April 20
May 20

Practical. Determined. Patient. Persevering. Doesn't like change. Down-to-earth. A loyal friend. Trustworthy. Obstinate.

Presidents born under Taurus: **Monroe, Buchanan, Grant, Truman**

 **PISCES**
February 19
March 20

A contradictory personality. Visionary. Mystic. Sometimes outgoing, sometimes brooding. Powerful need to help others.

Presidents born under Pisces: **Washington, Madison, Jackson, Cleveland**

 **GEMINI**
May 21
June 20

Eloquent in speech and writing. Keen observer. Charming. Witty. Talented. Good memory. Makes quick decisions. Wide interests.

President born under Gemini: **Kennedy**

Tidbits & Trivia

CANCER
June 22
July 22

69

Extremely intuitive. Actions based on feelings. Sensitive to criticism. Conventional. Conservative. Home-loving.

Presidents born under Cancer:
J. Q. Adams, Coolidge, Ford

LIBRA
September 23
October 22

Ω

Strives for harmony. Has sense of fair play. Dislikes the coarse and uncouth. Thoughtful. Even-tempered. Can see both sides.

Presidents born under Libra:
Hayes, Arthur, Eisenhower, Carter

LEO
July 23
August 22

Ω

Natural leader. Good powers of organization. Determined and forceful. Enthusiastic. Frank. Broadminded and fair. Generous.

Presidents born under Leo:
B. Harrison, Hoover

SCORPIO
October 23
November 21

M

Self-confident. Outspoken. Strong sex drive. Good friend. Easily angered. Sense of superiority. Trustworthy. Proud.

Presidents born under Scorpio:
J. Adams, Polk, Garfield, T. Roosevelt, Harding

VIRGO
August 23
September 22

m

Discriminating. Perfectionist. Inspires respect rather than affection. Critical of others. Highly analytical mind.

Presidents born under Virgo:
Taft, L. Johnson

SAGITTARIUS
November 22
December 21

↑

Makes friends easily. Genial. Charitable. Affectionate. Open. Feeling for personal freedom. Honest. Forgiving. Intuitive.

Presidents born under Sagittarius:
Van Buren, Taylor, Pierce

THE PRESIDENTS

"PEACEMAKER" TURNS MATCHMAKER

Widower President **John Tyler** was having some difficulty pursuing his romance with young Julia Gardiner. He proposed after seeing her only five times, and never in private, and she had told him at once, "No, no, no!"

But fate took a hand in the President's courtship. Tyler had invited Julia and her father, David Gardiner, former Senator from New York, to a splendid celebration on board the frigate *Princeton*. The special February 28, 1844, cruise was planned to commemorate the firing of the world's largest naval gun, the "Peacemaker," which would mark the occasion with three ceremonial blasts during the day.

All went as planned for the first two firings, and Julia and the President left the upper decks to enjoy a "sumptuous collation" and dancing in the salon.

Suddenly, a tremendous explosion rocked the ship, as the "Peacemaker" misfired, killing eight people, including Julia's father as well as the Secretary of State and Secretary of the Navy.

Learning of her father's death, Julia fainted into the President's arms and virtually remained there. They were married four months later on June 26, 1844.

The "May-December" match was a hit. They had their first child in 1846, when Tyler was 56, and their seventh (his fifteenth!) when the former President was 70.

PAULINE

The **William Howard Taft** family kept a cow.

The cow was a milk cow.

The cow grazed on the White House lawn.

The cow's name was Pauline Wayne.

ONLY ONE...

Only one President was the grandfather of a President. **William Henry Harrison** was **Benjamin Harrison's** grandfather.

VEEP "BLEEPS"

Hoover's Vice-President, Charles Curtis, didn't mind in the least being called "Indian Charlie." He was, in fact, very proud of the fact that he was half Indian.

Hubert Horatio Humphrey, **Johnson's** V.P., struggled cheerfully with his name all his life, answering to HHH, "Happy Hubert" and even "Hu-Bird," after all the "Birds" in **Johnson's** family. What he didn't like, however, was to be called "Gabby."

Other Vice-Presidents have found their public images equally frank. It was said that **FDR's** Vice-President, John Nance Garner, saved his best judgment for "picking the right Bourbon!"

Tidbits & Trivia

A COOLIDGE TAKES THE LEAD

The Spartan Coolidge homestead in Plymouth Notch, Vermont, where **Calvin Coolidge** was vacationing when President Harding died, was the scene of an extraordinary "lamplight inaugural" the night of August 3, 1923. In response to the news, Coolidge's father, a Notary Public, administered the Oath of Office at 2:47 A.M. Years later, when the former President's father was asked how he knew he could administer the oath to his son, Colonel Coolidge replied, "I didn't know that I couldn't."

TAFT LAFT

Although perennial presidential candidate Robert Taft was not known for his sense of humor, he did have one favorite true story he liked to tell to show that Congress was tolerant of all kinds of people:

"When Senator Smoot of Utah was elected to the Senate, there was a little consternation about having a Mormon in the Senate since Mormons still believed in polygamy. As soon as Utah achieved statehood and held its first election, a delegation of the righteous rushed to see an old political boss to voice their alarm.

"The political boss looked over the members of the delegation and spied one of them who was a notorious womanizer. Looking sternly at the culprit, he observed, 'I would much prefer a polygamist who doesn't polyg to a monogamist who doesn't monog.'"

CLEAN MIND, CLEAN BODY

Abigail Fillmore put her foot down. She wasn't moving into the White House until it was equipped with two things she refused to live without: A Bible and a bathtub. It was at her insistence that Congress cleaned up its act and finally appropriated funds for the White House's first library and indoor plumbing.

DIRE STRAITS

When President **Benjamin Harrison** moved into the White House in 1889, the First Family consisted of the President and Mrs. Harrison, a son and daughter, their mates and three offspring, Mrs. Harrison's old father, and her widowed niece — a total of eleven persons.

In 1889, the Executive Mansion was equipped with a single bathroom.

"Very few people," Mrs. Harrison remarked, "understand to what straits the President's family have been put at times for lack of accommodation."

NIGHT LIFE

Very few Presidents and First Ladies regularly slept in the same room at the White House, usually citing the varying schedules, midnight phone calls, and so forth, as the reasons. But the Trumans and the Fords were the exception.

"We've slept in the same bed for 25 years, and I see no reason to change now," Betty Ford told reporters with her usual candor.

THE PRESIDENTS

WHERE'S THE SMOKE?

The political term "smoke-filled room" originated with Harry Daugherty, **Warren Harding's** campaign manager prior to the 1920 Republican convention. Daugherty said, "I don't expect Senator Harding to be nominated on the first, second, or third ballots, but I think we can afford to take chances that, about eleven minutes after two, Friday morning of the convention, when ten or twenty weary men are sitting around a table, someone will say, 'Who will we nominate?' At that decisive time the friends of Harding will suggest him and we can afford to abide by the result."

Daugherty made no mention of smoke. Someone must have added that later.

TYLER'S WAY

Ex-President **John Tyler** was elected to the House of Representatives in 1861. This was truly the House divided against itself, for it was to the Confederate House of Representatives that Tyler, a Virginian, had been elected.

He was the only United States President to serve in the Confederate Government.

SHIFT OF EMPHASIS

For many years after its creation, the office of President of the United States was generally considered to be and was often referred to as that of Chief Magistrate.

THE MOST CONSECUTIVE EXECUTIVE

The 22nd Amendment to the Constitution provided that "no person shall be elected to the office of President more than twice."

This would seem to assure the longevity record of **Franklin D. Roosevelt,** who succeeded himself, and succeeded himself, and succeeded himself.

From March 4, 1932, until he died in office on April 12, 1945, FDR served a total of 4,422 days as President.

OLDEST, YOUNGEST

The oldest man to be inaugurated President of the United States was **Ronald Reagan,** 69 years old.

The oldest upon leaving the presidency was **Dwight Eisenhower,** who was 70.

The youngest elected President was **John Kennedy,** 43 at the time of his inauguration.

The youngest President, **Theodore Roosevelt,** was 42 when he assumed the office following the assassination of **William McKinley.**

When T. R.'s second term was over, he was still only 50 years old, making him the youngest ex-President.

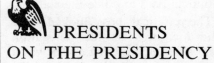 ## PRESIDENTS ON THE PRESIDENCY

The nearer I get to the inauguration of my successor, the greater the relief I feel.

William Howard Taft

Tidbits & Trivia

DOGS

Presidents generally are dog-owners. A lot more Presidents have had dogs than Presidents who haven't.

Washington, Jefferson, Madison, Monroe, William Henry Harrison, Tyler, Taylor, and **Polk** had dogs.

Jackson, Lincoln, both **Teddy** and **Franklin Roosevelt** had dogs. So did **Wilson** and **Harding** and **Coolidge** and **Hoover.**

Nixon had dogs. **Johnson** had dogs. **Kennedy** had dogs. **Eisenhower** had dogs. **Jerry Ford** had a dog.

Right from the beginning, the dogs have been going to the White House. Or you can put it the other way if you prefer.

PLAIN TALK FROM THE VEEP

President **Truman** was so quotable there wasn't much his Vice-President, Alben Barkley, could say, but he did make one notable comment to illustrate the poverty of his childhood. He said, "We were so poor that we had to use hoot owls for watchdogs."

VEEP TAKES A BRIDE

The first Vice-President to marry in office was Alben William Barkley, who late in life found love at last, when he tied the knot with a beautiful widow in her thirties, Elizabeth Jane Rucker, on November 18, 1948, in St. Louis, Missouri.

ACCORDING TO THE DEVIL'S DICTIONARY

One of American writer Ambrose Bierce's more ambitious efforts was a work he called "The Devil's Dictionary," in which he supplied Biercian definitions.

Among these:

PRESIDENCY — The greased pig in the field game of American politics.

COOLIDGE ON HOOVER

"That man," said President **Coolidge,** speaking of **Hoover,** "has offered me unsolicited advice for six years, all of it *bad!*"

MORE ABOUT DOGS

Herbert Hoover once issued an order that no staffer was to pet his dog, King Tut. Apparently, King Tut was becoming too accustomed to love and affection from everyone else, and began to ignore the President when he called. **Nixon** had similar trouble, but **Gerald Ford** and his dog, Liberty, were so close the President had no trouble in enlisting man's best friend for "undercover" work. When visitors lingered too long, Ford signaled Liberty, who padded into the Oval Office, providing a diversion that gave Ford an excuse to get up and cut short the conference.

THE PRESIDENTS

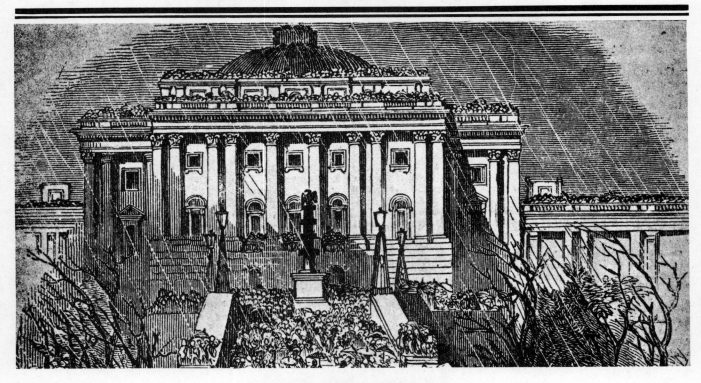

CAPITOL SUGGESTIONS

For centuries the story has persisted that the Capitol (which has been known to sink, swing and sway) is haunted by several unhappy spirits.

The first, a workman who argued with Benjamin Latrobe that a certain arch was not needed, was crushed to death when he began pulling out stones to prove his point. His dying words were a curse upon the Capitol.

Spirit number two is a stonemason, apparently killed in a fight with a carpenter during the building's construction and sealed into a wall with his own tools. You can't miss him. He's the transparent figure with a trowel in his hand who from time to time passes through a solid wall on the Senate side of the building.

The pathetic ghost of Pierre L'Enfant, laid to rest in a pauper's grave because he was never paid for laying out the Capital City, haunts the hall of the Capitol, a roll of plans carefully tucked under one arm.

Not to be outdone, **John Quincy Adams'** spirit stalks the Capitol, trying to finish his speech against the Mexican War, during which he suffered his fatal stroke.

Assassinated President **Garfield**, too, has paid a spiritual visit to the Rotunda, where his body lay in state, and his murderer has made a similar appearance.

SEND THE PIANO PLAYER HOME

Among presidential music lovers, **Ulysses S. Grant** was not one. Said Grant, "I only know two tunes. One of them is 'Yankee Doodle' and the other one isn't."

GUESS WHO?

Guess what President said, "Twice in my life I killed wild animals and I have regretted both acts ever since."

Ulysses S. Grant

Tidbits & Trivia

THE FIRST

The first President to ride on a railroad train was **Andrew Jackson,** in 1833.

THE FIRST

The first President born outside the 13 original states was **Abraham Lincoln.**

THE FIRST

The first President to ride on a steamship was **James Monroe.** The ship was the *Savannah,* and the date May 1819. A few weeks later the *Savannah* sailed for Europe and became the first American steamship to cross the Atlantic.

THE FIRST

The first girl born in the White House was Letitia Tyler, granddaughter of President **John Tyler.** Her parents were Tyler's son Robert and his wife Priscilla.

FINANCIAL STATEMENT

Andrew Jackson left the presidency with $90 in cash. His estate, The Hermitage, was thousands of dollars in debt.

He was 70 years old. It was time he got busy with the chores.

SOMEONE'S IN THE KITCHEN WITH ANDREW

The President's official cabinet is selected with the advice and consent of the Senate. There have been instances, however, when a President wished to have among his close advisers men whom the Senators, if asked, would have advised against having and not consented to. Many Presidents have gotten around this by making such men members of their "unofficial" cabinets.

Andrew Jackson surrounded himself by such a group. His enemies called them his "kitchen cabinet," presumably because they were men who came in through the back door and were close to all the goodies.

MAYBE THEY FINALLY ASKED HIS MOTHER

George Washington may have slept in more places than any other President, but **Andrew Jackson** was reportedly born in more places than any other Chief Executive.

Some of the spots that have vied for the honor of the General's birthplace are: Union County, North Carolina; Berkeley County, Virginia (now West Virginia); Augusta County, Virginia (now West Virginia); York County, Pennsylvania; England; Ireland; and the high seas.

For the record, Andy's actual birthplace is listed as Waxhaw, South Carolina.

THE PRESIDENTS

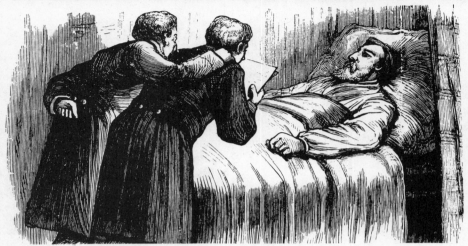

GOOD QUESTION

The Republican Party leaders were discussing who should run as Vice-President with their presidential candidate **Rutherford B. Hayes.** The name of William A. Wheeler was proposed to Hayes, who answered with a question that was admirable for its simplicity, its directness and its candor.

"Who is Wheeler?" asked Hayes.

HOW ABRAHAM LINCOLN FREED THE CORPORATION

Before he became President, **Abraham Lincoln** was a corporation lawyer. One of his clients was the Illinois Central Railroad. The railroad had a nice charter. Instead of paying taxes, it was permitted to pay a percentage of its earnings to the State of Illinois.

Then one of the Illinois counties, McLean by name, decided to tax the railroad, just like it taxed any other property. This was good for McLean, but paying taxes to every county that it ran through would have wrecked the railroad.

When the case came to trial in the Circuit Court, McLean County won it. Lincoln appealed to the State Supreme Court, argued his case twice, and in 1855 got a reversal, saving the Illinois Central untold millions and from almost certain bankruptcy.

Lincoln submitted his bill to the railroad. It was a healthy one but not unreasonable, considering how much he'd saved the corporation. The Illinois Central, however, thought the fee was outrageous and paid Lincoln $200.

ALL FOR OUR COUNTRY

Oh, well, back to the courtroom. Abe decided he now wanted $5,000 for his efforts, part of it for winning the case, the rest for collecting his fee. He sued for that amount, argued his own case, and the jury awarded him the $5,000. Did the railroad pay? Not until an order was issued for the sheriff to confiscate railroad property if it didn't. That's how Abe finally got his money. Until the bitter end, the good old Illinois Central felt it had been taken for a ride by a country lawyer.

TALE OF THREE CITIES

New York, Philadelphia and Washington, D. C., have each served as capital of the United States. **George Washington** was the only President to be inaugurated in two of them, New York and Philadelphia, and the only Chief Executive who did not live in Washington, D. C. **Thomas Jefferson** was the first President to be inaugurated there, for **John Adams** took the oath of office in Philadelphia.

Tidbits & Trivia

HOW TO ECONOMIZE WITHOUT REALLY TRYING

During World War II Eleanor Roosevelt's kitchen economies caught the attention of the Food Administration, which considered them adaptable to "other large households." The *New York Times* rhapsodized:

"Mrs. Roosevelt does the shopping, the cooks see that there is no food wasted, the laundress is sparing in her use of soap, each servant has a watchful eye for evidence of shortcomings on the part of others; and all are encouraged to make helpful use of 'left overs.'"

According to the reporter, Mrs. Roosevelt said, "Making ten servants help me to do my saving has not only been possible but highly profitable."

Franklin Roosevelt, along with the rest of Washington, was highly amused. He wrote:

"All I can say is that your latest newspaper campaign is a corker and I am proud to be the husband of the Originator, Discoverer and Inventor of the New Household Economy for Millionaires! Please have a photo taken showing the family, the ten cooperating servants, the scraps saved from the table and the hand book. I will have it published in the Sunday *Times*."

GOOD CHOICE

During World War II, Eleanor Roosevelt traveled extensively. In order to maintain security when she was communicating with the President during these trips, she had been assigned a code name. The frequency of her travels had suggested the choice. Mrs. Roosevelt's code name was Rover.

WOMEN'S HOUR

The first First Lady ever to cast a vote in a presidential election was Eleanor Roosevelt, who was voter number 203 on Election Day, 1920, at Hyde Park, New York. It's a good bet she was voting for her husband, who was on the ballot running for Vice-President.

ALL-IN-THE-FAMILY WEDDING

Eleanor Roosevelt's father, Elliot, was dead when she became engaged to her fifth cousin, Franklin. At her wedding she was given away by her father's brother, Uncle Teddy, the President. As he wrote to his son, Kermit, a few days later,

"I paid a scuttling visit to New York on Friday to give away Eleanor at her marriage, and to make two speeches — one to the Friendly Sons of St. Patrick and one to the Sons of the American Revolution."

A typically quiet day for Uncle Teddy.

THE PRESIDENTS

BY ANY OTHER NAME

Given names sometimes appear to fit a major facet of a person's character. We've all met a Dennis or two whose reverence for his namesake, Dionysus, [god of wine] was a bit excessive, or an Iris [rainbow] whose iridescence was quite visible. In a similar way, causation or not, some Presidents have first name meanings which matchup in an uncanny way, as in the following:

George [the farmer] Washington
Andrew [manly] Jackson
Abraham [high father] Lincoln
William [desirer of protection] McKinley
Theodore [born ruler] Roosevelt
Warren [an enclosure of animals that are by nature wild] Harding
Calvin [bald one] Coolidge

Harry [ruler of the house] Truman
John [the Lord is gracious] Kennedy
Gerald [spear carrier] Ford

But there are others like the two below which are somewhat ambiguous.

Herbert [glory of the army] Hoover
Richard [strong in rule] Nixon

And if one considers the 1980 election, what can be made of these?

Ronald [wise power] Reagan
Edward [guardian of wealth] Kennedy
James [variant of Jacob, he who overreaches] Carter

WORDS, WORDS, WORDS

The shortest inauguration speech, only 133 words, was delivered by **George Washington** at his second inaugural on March 4, 1793.

The longest, delivered by **William Henry Harrison** on March 4, 1841, contained 8,443 words.

At a normal speaking rate, Washington's speech lasted for about two minutes, Harrison's speech for an hour and ten minutes.

The fact that the longest speech preceded the shortest presidential term was no coincidence. Harrison delivered his message outdoors, on the east portico of the Capitol. In spite of the cold and stormy day, Harrison refused to wear a hat or coat. Harrison caught a cold, the cold developed into pneumonia, and Harrison died a month later.

THE FIRST

The first President to have his photograph taken in office was **William Henry Harrison,** in 1841.

Tidbits & Trivia

MOST ATHLETIC FIRST LADY?

Bess Truman was a star athlete of her class in finishing school. She said the training was invaluable to her as First Lady, because she could shake more hands than anyone else. Bess also beat daughter Margaret regularly at tennis. The White House staff, observing the Truman family flicking watermelon seeds at one another after a particularly hilarious dinner, complimented the First Lady on her aim. "Bess never missed," they said.

GIVE US A "B"
GIVE US AN "E"
GIVE US AN "S"
GIVE US ANOTHER "S"

When Bess Truman was a girl at boarding school, she participated in a track meet and won her event: the shotput.

SPEECH IMPROVEMENT

A very proper friend of Bess Truman was sympathizing with the very proper First Lady over the President's excessive use of the word "manure." Bess Truman looked at her friend coolly. "It took me twenty years to get him to say 'manure'."

TRADE SECRET

Calvin Coolidge gave the following advice for handling White House visitors to incoming President Herbert Hoover.

"If you keep dead still," he said, "they will run down in three or four minutes. If you even cough or smile, they will start up all over again."

SPEAKER LEARNS WHEN NOT TO

Speaker of the House Sam Rayburn credited **Calvin Coolidge** with saying the smartest thing he'd ever heard outside of the Bible.

"I found out early in life," Coolidge said, "That you don't have to explain something you haven't said."

KNOW YOUR LIMITATIONS

After being inaugurated, **Calvin Coolidge** said, "It is a great advantage to a President, and a major source of safety to the country for him to know that he is not a great man."

He cautioned, "When a man begins to feel that he is the only one who can lead in this republic, he is guilty of treason to the spirit of our institutions."

YANKEE DOODLE DANDY

Calvin Coolidge, a man who swung to his own tune, was the only President to be born on the Fourth of July. The year was 1872.

TRIM WHEREVER YOU CAN — C.C.

THE PRESIDENTS

THE FIRST

The first assassination attempt on a President occurred in 1835. Holding two pistols, a man named Richard Lawrence, who believed that **Andrew Jackson** was keeping him from his rightful position as King of America, confronted Jackson in the Capitol. Lawrence fired both pistols at close range. Both misfired. Lawrence was seized, adjudged insane, and committed to an asylum.

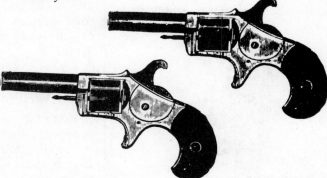

IT WAS A GREAT SPEECH, EVEN IF IT DID HAVE SOME HOLES IN IT

On October 14, 1912, while campaigning as the "Bull Moose" party candidate for a third presidential term, **Theodore Roosevelt** was in Milwaukee, Wisconsin, to make a speech. A Milwaukee resident named Shrank did not want Roosevelt to be President again, or even to make the speech. Shrank shot at the ex-President from close range. His bullet passed through Roosevelt's eyeglass case and through the manuscript of the speech, which was folded in his pocket. The speech was a long one and the manuscript was thick.

The bullet penetrated Roosevelt's chest but did no vital damage. The thick manuscript had slowed the velocity of the bullet. The speech had saved his life.

Being a gritty fellow, Roosevelt proceeded to deliver the speech despite the injury. He was glad that he had not chosen to say just a few words.

A WAITING AUDIENCE

The presidency of **Ronald Reagan** had hardly begun when on March 30, 1981, a would-be assassin fired a bullet which struck the President in the chest. Reagan was rushed to George Washington Hospital. As he was being wheeled into the operating room, the former actor, now President, looked up at the surgeons waiting for him and said half jokingly, "Please tell me you're all Republicans."

Tidbits & Trivia

EGO-DEFLATING

To a group of Nobel Prize winners attending a White House dinner, **John Kennedy** made this toast:

"I believe this is the most extraordinary collection of talent, of human knowledge, that has ever been gathered together at the White House, with the possible exception of when **Thomas Jefferson** dined alone."

ONLY ONE BEN

Benjamin Franklin served brilliantly as American ambassador to France. **Thomas Jefferson,** who followed Franklin in the post, was received by the Comte de Vergennes.

"You replace Dr. Franklin?" inquired the French count.

"No one can replace Franklin," replied Jefferson. "I merely succeed him."

THREE ON THE FOURTH

Of the first five Presidents, three died on the Fourth of July. In fact, two of them — **John Adams** and **Thomas Jefferson** — died only a few hours apart on the same day, July 4, 1826.

Having been Jefferson's lifelong political adversary, Adams remained competitive until the end. His last words were, "Thomas Jefferson still survives." But the last one belonged to John, for Jefferson had died earlier in the day.

Five years later, on July 4, 1831, **James Monroe** died.

TWO FOR THE DECLARATION, TWO FOR THE CONSTITUTION

While most of the early Presidents were active in the founding of the nation, only two of them signed the Declaration of Independence and two others the Constitution.

Thomas Jefferson and **John Adams** were signers of the Declaration of Independence.

George Washington and **James Madison** were the Presidents who signed the Constitution.

WANTED: ONE WHITE HOUSE

Fittingly, the original design for the White House was selected by means of an open competition. The plan submitted by Irish-born architect James Hoban was chosen. His prize for the winning entry was $500 and a city lot.

The announcement for the competition had been written by **Thomas Jefferson.** Among the losers was a design submitted by an anonymous "A. Z.", who later was discovered to be an amateur architect named Thomas Jefferson.

SHE'D HAD PRACTICE

Dolley Madison was one of the most successful First Ladies. There was a good reason for this. Prior to husband James' term of office, she had served as official White House hostess for his predecessor, **Thomas Jefferson,** a widower.

THE FIRST

The first child born in the White House was James Madison Randolph, **Thomas Jefferson's** grandson. His mother was Jefferson's daughter Martha. James was her eighth child.

PRESIDENTS ON THE PRESIDENCY

"Never did a prisoner released from his chains feel such relief as I shall on shaking off the shackles of power."

Thomas Jefferson

THE PRESIDENTS

BEARDING THE LION

Historians speculate that one reason **Lincoln** grew a beard was this charming note from Grace Bedell, a little girl from New York who wrote in October 1860:

. . . . ."I have got 4 brothers and part of them will vote for you anyway and if you will let your whiskers grow I will try and get the rest of them to vote for you you would look a great deal better for your face is so thin. All the ladies like whiskers and they would tease their husbands to vote for you and then you would be President."

In a letter headed "Private," Lincoln responded:

"My dear little Miss.

Your very agreeable letter of the 15th is received — I regret the necessity of saying I have no daughters — I have three sons — one seventeen, one nine, and one seven years of age — They, with their mother, constitute my whole family —

As to the whiskers, having never worn any, do you not think people would call it a piece of silly affection if I were to begin it now?

Your very sincere well-wisher
A. Lincoln"

The letter was dated October 19, 1860. That fall, his "whiskers" began to grow.

BRIGHT BOY YOU'VE GOT THERE

At the age of nine, **John Quincy Adams** wrote the following letter to his father.

Dear Sir, —

I love to receive letters very well; much better than I love to write them. I make but a poor figure at composition. My head is much too fickle. My thoughts are running after bird's eggs, play and trifles, till I get vexed with myself. Mama has a troublesome task to keep me a studying. I own I am ashamed of myself. I have but just entered the third volume of Smollet, but designed to have got half through it by this time. I am determined this week to be more diligent. Mr. Thaxter is absent at Court. I have set myself a stint this week, to read the third volume half out. If I can but keep my resolution, I may again at the end of the week give a better account of myself. I wish, sir, you would give me in writing, some instructions with regard to the use of my time, and advise me how to proportion my studies and play, and I will keep them by me, and endeavor to follow them.

With the present determination of growing better, I am, dear sir, your son,

John Quincy Adams

Five years later, the 14-year-old future President was serving as private secretary to the American minister to Russia.

PLACES, PLEASE

The election of 1884 matched Republican James G. Blaine against Democrat **Grover Cleveland.**

Neither candidate had unsoiled political linen. Blaine, in his official position as Speaker of the House, had engaged in some highly questionable stock manipulation. Cleveland's reputation was sullied by an illicit sexual exploit, complete with offspring.

This presented a dilemma to the voters, the solution to which was suggested, at the time, as follows:

"We are told that Mr. Blaine has been delinquent in office but blameless in private life, while Mr. Cleveland has been a model of official integrity but culpable in his personal relations. We should therefore elect Mr. Cleveland to the public office which he is so qualified to fill and remand Mr. Blaine to the private station which he is so admirably fitted to adorn."

1. THE BUG
2. THE CURE

"When the presidential bug gets into your veins," said Senator George Aiken of Vermont, "the only thing that will get it out is embalming fluid."

DANGER ALL AROUND

Until the latter part of the 1800s, among the difficulties faced by men who became President was a very basic one . . . living in Washington.

The nation's capital was built on low, marshy ground. Garbage disposal was handled largely, albeit unofficially, by a wandering corps of pigs. Muddy streets and stagnant canals, high humidity and penetrating dampness all were part of the Washingtonian ambience. The city was also a magnificent breeding ground for various diseases. For malaria-carrying mosquitoes, Washington, particularly around the Potomac River, was a splendid place to live, and many of them did. The presidential practice of vacating the White House for the summer was not simply to vacation. It was defensive.

In 1881, Mrs. James Garfield got out of town too late. That year the malaria mosquitoes attacked in the spring and bit, among others, the First Lady. She came down with an attack of malaria.

While Mrs. Garfield recuperated at the family home at Elberon, New Jersey, her husband, James, stayed on in humid Washington to attend a college reunion. On July 2, as he prepared to leave from Union Station in Washington, the President was assassinated.

It was a very bad year for Mrs. Garfield.

THE PRESIDENTS

FROM ATOM TO EAT 'EM

Jimmy Carter is the only President to have been commander of both a nuclear submarine and a peanut farm.

EIGHT IS ENOUGH

When **Grover Cleveland** took office in March of 1893, he was joined by eight George Washingtons in Congress. There were three from Ohio, George Washington Houk, Hulick and Wilson; two from Illinois, George Washington Smith and Fithian; two from South Carolina, George Washington Shell and Murray; and George Washington Ray from New York.

THAT TOO?

Only one President has ever received a patent. Anyone who knows anything about Presidents would expect that the man must be the inventive Thomas Jefferson. But it wasn't.

On May 29, 1849, a patent for lifting vessels more easily over shoals by inflating air chambers near the water line was issued to **Abraham Lincoln.** He got the idea from personal experience with the problem during a flatboat trip down the Mississippi River.

So far as is known, the invention never got much past the patent stage, or the building of a model, a copy of which can be seen in the museum at Ford's Theater in Washington.

A TRULY BIG MAN

When **William Howard Taft** died, Will Rogers paid him this tribute:

"Mr. Taft! What a lovely soul! Just as a man and a real honest-to-God fellow, Mr. Taft will go to his grave with more real downright affection and less enemies than any of our Presidents.

"It's great to be great but it's greater to be human. He was our great human fellow because there was more of him to be human. We are parting with three hundred pounds of solid charity to everybody, and love and affection for all his fellow men."

THE FIRST

The first President to have been divorced was **Ronald Reagan.** His first marriage to Jane Wyman ended in divorce in 1948.

THREE TO GET READY

When **Abe Lincoln** appointed Charles Francis Adams Minister to Great Britain in March of 1861, he was just continuing a family tradition. Charles Francis' father, **John Quincy Adams,** and his grandfather, **John Adams,** had both served in the same post.

ONE-MAN YELLOW PAGES

Thomas Jefferson can be described simply, in these words:

anthropologist
architect
bibliophile
botanist
classicist
diplomat
educator
ethnologist
farmer
geographer
gourmet
horseman
horticulturist
inventor
lawyer
lexicographer
linguist
mathematician
meteorologist
naturalist
numismatist
paleontologist
philosopher
politician
statesman
violinist
writer

Tidbits & Trivia

YOU COULD BANK ON HER

The first First Lady to hold a job other than the genteel position of tutor or teacher was Ida McKinley, who worked as a bank cashier.

But it was no disgrace; it was her father's bank.

TOKEN OF APPRECIATION

Shortly after he became President, **John Kennedy** publicly thanked Clark Clifford, the Washington lawyer who had helped to effect a smooth transition between the outgoing Eisenhower administration and Kennedy's.

At a dinner party, he said of Clifford, "Clark helped us a great deal and asked for only one small favor in return . . . that we advertise his law firm on the back of one-dollar bills."

WASTE NOT, WANT NOT

LBJ was one of the first to be conscious of an energy-saving image, turning off lights in the White House that **Nixon** later turned on. Like Johnson, who watched the wattage at his ranch as well, President **Ford** was careful about the lights, at home and at the office.

He also drove his staff crazy wearing pencils down to tiny stubs before he would take a new one.

I'VE GROWN ACCUSTOMED TO THE FACE

Portraits of Presidents appear on our paper money. Sometimes bills of high denominations honor Presidents of less than stellar rank. It is one case where a Ulysses S. Grant is worth 50 George Washingtons.

The greenback picture gallery includes:

$1 bill — **George Washington**
$2 bill — **Thomas Jefferson**
$5 bill — **Abraham Lincoln**
$20 bill — **Andrew Jackson**
$50 bill — **Ulysses S. Grant**

Still in use as legal tender but no longer being printed are:

$500 bill — **William McKinley**
$1000 bill — **Grover Cleveland**
$5000 bill — **James Madison**

Three non-Presidents complete the series: Alexander Hamilton on the $10 bill, Benjamin Franklin on the $100 bill, and Salmon P. Chase on the $10,000 bill.

The images of Presidents in our billfolds are beginning to fade, however. It is an eclipse due to greater use of checks and credit cards (the decreased value of U.S. dollars is a different kind of fading).

Portraits of six Presidents grace United States coins now in circulation. In our coin-operated times the demand exceeds supply. The **Eisenhower** silver dollar, first issued in 1971, is the most recent portrait coin to honor a late President. The other presidential coins in reverse order of appearance are: the **Kennedy** half-dollar (1964), the **Roosevelt** dime (1946), the **Jefferson** nickel (1938), the **Washington** quarter (1932), and the **Lincoln** penny (1909). The new, small-sized Susan B. Anthony dollar, the only non-presidential coin now being minted, is having trouble gaining acceptance. Too bad, though, for she probably would have made a good President, or at the very least better than some we've had.

THE PRESIDENTS

GIRLS WILL BE GIRLS

Woodrow Wilson's daughters, Margaret, Jessie, and Eleanor, enjoyed living in the White House. These young ladies especially liked to join White House guided tours, keeping their identity secret from the tourists. As the guide showed the out-of-town visitors through the Executive Mansion, the girls would embarrass their fellow tour members by making loud and highly critical remarks about President Wilson's daughters.

IT'S NOT WHAT YOU SAY, BUT THE WAY THAT YOU SAY IT

President **Kennedy's** inaugural comments, "Ask not what your country can do for you, but ask what you can do for your country," echoed around the world. They were not, however, his words, but those of another President: **Warren G. Harding**.

"...ALL [WO]MEN ARE CREATED EQUAL..."

A convention of seceders and unauthorized delegates in 1872 nominated the first female candidate for President, Victoria Claflin Woodhull.

At the same gathering, Frederick Douglass was nominated for Vice President, the first black so nominated.

The renegades later took the inflammatory name of the Equal Rights Party.

THE FIRST

The first presidential radio broadcast was made by **Warren Harding** in June of 1922 at the dedication of the Francis Scott Key Memorial at Fort McHenry, Baltimore, Maryland.

ROAD TO HEALTH.

Up in the Morning Early.

HERE SHE GOES, THERE SHE GOES.

WHAT EVERY WOMAN *REALLY* KNOWS

Jackie Kennedy captivated many men, even as a young "Inquiring Camera Girl" journalist on Capitol Hill. One of them was William "Fishbait" Miller, Congressional Doorkeeper, who even offered to help her with her romance with the exciting young Senator from Massachusetts. First, he warned her to "keep hands off" the party's most glamorous and eligible man. Then he said, "But if you really want him, Jackie, I'll help you get him."

"Fishbait, you nut," she replied. "If I need help, I'll advertise."

LOVE IN BLOOM

Tricia Nixon's Rose Garden wedding at the White House was the first outdoor nuptial in the history of the Pennsylvania Avenue mansion.

Naturally, it rained.

Tidbits & Trivia

A LEG MAN

Pat Nixon, credited by reporters with "the best legs" of any First Lady, always wore skirts, but not necessarily to show off her legs.

Her husband, it seemed, preferred them. "Slacks can do something for some people and some it can't," he said. "Every time I see a girl in slacks it reminds me of China."

IT'S IN THE STARS

While the White House has always been host to countless celebrities, modern Presidents have all had their special favorites. Pearl Bailey was **Nixon's** favorite and also **Gerald Ford's**; **Lyndon Johnson** liked Carol Channing; **Harry Trun 1** preferred the singing of his daughter Margaret, and **Ike** admired Robert Montgomery. **Cal Coolidge** liked Will Rogers, who said about him, "He didn't do nothing, but that's what we wanted done."

HER FATHER'S DAUGHTER?

Tricia Nixon was considered the ultraconservative in the family, with one reporter describing her as "slightly to the right of Genghis Khan."

Nixon himself admitted that she was right wing, "but not on the kooky right."

Asked if she was going to convert her fiancé, Ed Cox, Democrat and former "Nader Raider," to the Republican party, she said, "I don't think I need do any proselytizing."

"ONE FROM COLUMN A AND TWO FROM COLUMN B"

The very straightlaced **Herbert Hoovers** occasionally spoke to each other in Chinese in front of White House guests so no one would know what they were discussing.

ART APPRECIATION

One of the most admired portraits in the White House is that of **Calvin Coolidge's** wife, Grace. The artist, Howard Chandler Christie, had Mrs. Coolidge pose for the painting in a red dress with her white collie at her side.

When the painting was shown to President Coolidge, he didn't like it. Everything was all right except for the red dress. He preferred her in white. It was pointed out to him that a white dress would not have provided sufficient contrast with the white collie. The President acknowledged the artist's problem and supposed it had been cheaper to buy the new dress than to dye the dog.

THE PRESIDENTS

BUILD YOUR OWN CABIN WITH A FULL-SIZED SET OF LINCOLN LOGS

Log cabins and homespun Presidents are inextricably linked to our nation's fondness for rusticity and frontier vigor. No other President is more closely tied to his log cabin beginnings than **Abraham Lincoln.**

Our sixteenth President was born in 1809, in a small, one-room log cabin a few miles south of Hodgenville, Kentucky. That humble dwelling on the section of property near Sinking Spring may have been built by Abraham's father, Thomas Lincoln. The Lincolns lived there two more years, clearing the land of trees to make a farm. Then, as the result of a land-title dispute, they moved to a new location, on Knobs Creek, about 6 miles northeast of Hodgenville. There is no mention of moving the cabin timbers for the new home. In later years, Abraham stated that that rude cabin at Sinking Spring was the first home he could recall.

In 1894, almost thirty years after the death of Lincoln, someone finally remembered the Lincoln log cabin in the woods. A certain Alfred W. Dennett, a restaurateur and philanthropist (?) of New York, purchased 110 acres of the property where Thomas Lincoln's farm once stood, hoping to create a Lincoln birthplace tourist mecca. Dennett couldn't find the original structure, but he did locate an aging log cabin standing on nearby property that, according to local tradition, incorporated some of the same notched logs that had been used in the Lincoln cabin. The logs (Lincoln-made, or a reasonable facsimile) were reerected at the approximate location of Thomas's cabin.

Apparently Dennett's plans were not the commercial success he expected, for in 1897 he dismantled the cabin and transported it to Tennessee, where it was reassembled and displayed to crowds at the Nashville Centennial celebration. After that the logs were placed in storage in New York City and remained there until 1901, when they were unpacked and shipped to Buffalo for that city's Pan-American Exposition. After the end of the Exposition (which lost both money and a President in the assassination of **McKinley**), the cabin was knocked down again for return to storage. Some logs were lost in transit; the rest remained untouched for several years in the cellar of an old mansion at College Point on Long Island.

This neglect could not long endure; the true worth of a full-sized set of Lincoln logs was finally recognized and America's need to see presidential birthplaces, at last, could be satisfied by the arrival of the motor car. In 1906, the Lincoln Farm Association acquired the birthplace site and the logs. While a permanent memorial shelter was being constructed at the birthplace site, one more road-show installation was put on at Louisville, Kentucky.

The logs were reassembled (hopefully for the final time) within a large Greek revival structure of pink and white marble at the old Sinking Spring site. President **Taft** took part in the dedication ceremony held on November 9, 1909. The rude cabin was home at last and protected from all the wind and rain, much as it had sheltered the young Lincoln.

Tidbits & Trivia

LYNDA MAKES WAVES

An enterprising journalist, Lynda Bird Johnson set off on a North Country canoe trip for *National Geographic*. An equally enterprising press crew in hot pursuit soon found Lynda in floppy hat and dark glasses, dubbing her the "Greta Garbo of the North Woods," and dogging her trail unceasingly.

Lynda kept them at bay, however, refusing all interviews and maintaining a solitary camp on the riverbank. Then, a bourbon bottle with note inside washed up at her campsite. Launched by footsore reporters, the note inside the bottle read:

"We four sunburned, mosquito-bitten muscle-sore members of the press have tried to respect your desire for privacy on this trip. But as the sun sets on the last evening of the canoe voyage, we are beginning to worry more and more about our editors back home. Could you spare a few minutes to chat with us?"

Suddenly, "Greta" arrived. "Your message was so ingenious, I just couldn't resist coming over," said Lynda, granting what became known as "The Bourbon Bottle Press Conference."

FIRST LADY ON FIRST LADIES

Jackie Kennedy said her favorite First Lady was Bess Truman, for whom she had the "most affinity" because "she brought a daughter to the White House at a most difficult age and managed to keep her from being spoiled."

HELP SEND A BOY TO CAMP

Lou Hoover was an outdoor girl, and she thought a rustic retreat would be just the ticket for her beleaguered husband, up to his eyebrows in work trying to stem the Depression's tide. She planned a camp on the Rapidan River, designing even the furniture for a summer hideaway in the Virginia woods.

The forerunner of such famous presidential retreats as Camp David, Hoover's "summer place" in the Blue Ridge Mountains was later donated by the former President, who had paid for its construction out of his own pocket, to the Shenandoah National Park.

THE PRESIDENTS

OK, MARTIN

Martin Van Buren's nickname was Old Kinderhook, a reference to his hometown, Kinderhook, New York. O.K., the abbreviation of his nickname, was used as a Van Buren political slogan. Many experts in that kind of thing agree this is how the term originated.

WHAD HE SAY?

They didn't call **Martin Van Buren** the Fox of Kinderhook, the little Magician, and the American Talleyrand for nothing. A consummate politician, pleasant, smooth, personable, and deft, he was highly adept at the arts of fence-sitting and non-committalism.

Nowhere were his skills better demonstrated than they were at Albany, New York, on July 10, 1827, before a group of wool growers and manufacturers.

The matter in question was a tariff. The gentlemen in the audience were unanimously in favor of a high protective tariff on imported woolens. In the South, the feeling was strongly against the tariff. As policy-maker for the Democratic Party, Van Buren's job was to keep both sides happy. The Fox was equal to the occasion.

He spoke for an hour and the speech was received with enthusiasm.

When Van Buren had finished speaking, one wool buyer turned to a friend.

"Mr. Knower, that was a very able speech."

"Yes," agreed Knower, "very able."

"Mr. Knower, on which side of the tariff question was it?"

DID HE HAVE A CRYSTAL BALL?

Political kingmaker Mark Hanna urged **William McKinley** to put someone other than **Theodore Roosevelt** on the ticket with him as Vice-President, telling Republican leaders:

"To make Roosevelt Vice-President would place but a single life between this madman and the presidency."

However, Hanna's advice was ignored at the Convention, T.R. became McKinley's Vice-President, and McKinley's assassination put T.R. in the White House.

His daughter said, "He's always wanted to be President. Now he *is* President. Hurrah, for Daddy!"

WHEN IS A WHITE HOUSE NOT A WHITE HOUSE?

It was popularly referred to as the White House from the very beginning. It also was called the President's Palace, the Executive Mansion, and the President's House, but the building had no official status until **Theodore Roosevelt** became a resident. He had the return address on his presidential stationery printed: The White House.

Since it was official stationery, the name somehow became official, too, and generally has been accepted as such ever since.

Tidbits & Trivia

RINGLING BROTHERS, BARNUM & ROOSEVELT

"I don't think any family has ever enjoyed the White House more than we have," wrote **Teddy Roosevelt.** No one has ever been known to dispute the statement.

There were pillow fights, father included. which TR described as "vigorous."

There was stilt walking and bicycle riding in the halls, and why were those spiral lines and broad ruts covering the parquet oak flooring of the East Room?

"We thought it would make a fine roller skating rink," said the children, "and we found it dandy."

There were wrestling matches, of both a domestic and imported variety. "I am wrestling with two Japanese wrestlers three times a week," wrote Teddy. "My right ankle and my left wrist and one thumb and both great toes are swollen sufficiently to more or less impair their usefulness, and I am well mottled with bruises elsewhere. Still I have made good progress, and . . . they have taught me three new throws that are perfect corkers."

And then there was the menagerie. This included dogs, cats, rabbits, guinea pigs, squirrels, raccoons, a badger, a black bear, a kangaroo rat, TR Jr.'s parrot, Eli, and Alice's green garter snake, Emily Spinach . . . "Emily" in honor of a skinny aunt and "Spinach" for its color.

Perhaps the favorite pet was their calico pony, Algonquin. When Archie was confined to his second-floor bedroom with the measles, the only thing his brothers could think of that would cheer up Archie was a visit from Algonquin. So Algonquin paid Archie a visit. And how did the pony get up to the second floor? Foolish question. He rode up on the elevator like anybody else.

THE PRESIDENTS

White House

President

Frances Folsom
daughter of
Emma Cornelia Harmon Folsom and Oscar Folsom
to
Grover Cleveland
son of
Anne Neal Cleveland and Richard Falley Cleveland
June 2, 1886

Presidents' Daughters

Maria Hester Monroe
daughter of
President and Mrs. James Monroe
to
Samuel Lawrence Gouverneur
March 9, 1820

Elizabeth Tyler
daughter of
President and Mrs. John Tyler
to
William Nevison Waller
January 31, 1842

Nellie Grant
daughter of
President and Mrs. Ulysses Simpson Grant
to
Algernon Frederick Sartoris
May 21, 1874

Alice Lee Roosevelt
daughter of
President Theodore Roosevelt and the late
Mrs. Alice Hathaway Lee Roosevelt
to
Representative Nicholas Longworth
February 17, 1906

Tidbits & Trivia

Weddings

Jessie Woodrow Wilson
daughter of
President and Mrs. Woodrow Wilson
to
Francis Bowes Sayre
November 25, 1913

Eleanor Randolph Wilson
daughter of
President and Mrs. Woodrow Wilson
to
Secretary of the Treasury William Gibbs McAdoo
May 7, 1914

Lynda Bird Johnson
daughter of
President and Mrs. Lyndon Baines Johnson
to
Captain Charles Spitall Robb, USMC
December 9, 1967

Patricia Nixon
daughter of
President and Mrs. Richard Milhous Nixon
to
Edward Finch Cox
June 12, 1971

President's Son

Mary Catherine Hellen
to
John Adams
son of
President and Mrs. John Quincy Adams
February 25, 1828

POETIC GIFT

When President Grant's daughter, Nellie, married a dashing Englishman, Algernon Charles Frederick Sartoris, the most unusual gift the newlyweds received was this poem, written especially for the occasion by Walt Whitman:

A KISS FOR THE BRIDE

Sacred, blithesome, undenied
With benisons from East and West
And salutations North and South.
Through me indeed today a
*   million hearts and hands*
Wafting a million loves, a million
*   soul-felt prayers:*
— Tender and true remain the
*   arm that shields thee!*
*   Fair winds always fill the sails*
*   that sail thee!*
*   Clear sun by day, and bright*
*   star at night beam on thee!*
Dear girl — through me the
*   ancient privilege too*
For the New World, through me,
*   the old, old wedding greeting:*
O youth and health! O sweet
*   Missouri rose! O bonny bride!*
Yield thy red cheeks, thy lips,
*   today*
Unto a Nation's loving kiss.

Nice thought, but Walt's good wishes didn't help. Sartoris turned out to be a drunk, and after a few years Nellie left him.

THE PRESIDENTS

THE MAKING
OF A PRESIDENT
1840

Before the Whigs nominated **William Henry Harrison** for President in 1836, Nicholas Biddle, Director of the Bank of the United States, advised Harrison's managers, "Say not one single word about his principles or his creed. Let him say nothing, promise nothing. Let no committee, no convention, no town meeting ever extract from him a single word about what he thinks now and will do hereafter. Let the use of pen and ink be wholly forbidden."

Although Harrison lost the election to Martin Van Buren, all agreed it had been sound political advice. The managers remembered it four years later when Harrison was nominated again. The only problem was it didn't leave them much to work with.

An article which appeared in a Baltimore newspaper supplied the angle they needed. Following Harrison's nomination, it commented of the candidate: "Give him a barrel of hard cider and a pension of $2,000 a year and he will sit the remainder of his days in a log cabin by the side of a 'sea coal' fire and study moral philosophy."

Log cabin! Hard cider! That's it! Whether Harrison, who had been born in a three-story brick mansion in Virginia, had ever been inside a log cabin, or tasted hard cider, for that matter, was quite beside the point.

You, there. It's your job to keep Harrison quiet. Now, boys, let's get started. You fellows are the log cabin committee. Get going on the log cabin song books, the floats, the clubs, the badges, the posters, the almanacs and the coonskin caps. And we want plenty of smoke coming from those chimneys. The rest of you are the hard cider committee. Put someone in charge of barrels.

We've been working all night on the slogan. Listen to this:

"Tippecanoe and Tyler too"

What? Oh, Tippecanoe is a river out in Indiana where General Harrison fought some Indians. Of course, he won. Killed about 30 Indians and he only had 180 casualties. And fortunately we've got Tyler running for Vice-President. Why? Because his name begins with T and it's short.

We'll need one more committee. A knock-the-opposition committee. Who wants to volunteer? Fine. Remember the battle cry. Van Buren sleeps in a French bed, eats with gold spoons, and uses finger bowls. Boys, how can we lose?

They didn't. And it wasn't even close.

BE IT EVER SO HUMBLE . . .

Being born in a log cabin surely had its disadvantages. Politically, however, it was a decided asset, as seven Presidents were to discover. In addition to **Abraham Lincoln,** they were: **Andrew Jackson, Zachary Taylor, Millard Fillmore, James Buchanan and James Garfield.** There were other presidential claimants to such primitive beginnings but the shelters where they first saw the light of day exceed true log cabin specifications.

Tidbits & Trivia

BUY A TICKET FOR THOMAS

On the face of the ticket there appeared these words:

"This ticket will entitle the holder thereof to such prize money as may be drawn to its numbers in the JEFFERSON LOTTERY."

In 1826, **Thomas Jefferson** was so deeply in debt that a public lottery was planned on his behalf. The lottery never was held. Friends of Jefferson were able, instead, to raise the thousands of dollars needed to save the ex-President from bankruptcy and enable him to spend his last days in peace and solvency at Monticello.

HAVE AN EGG-ROLL

Rutherford B. Hayes' wife, Lucy, loved children. When Congressmen complained that the annual Easter egg-rolling festivities, which until that time had been conducted at the Capitol, were ruining the national grass, Lucy had the activity moved to the White House lawn.

The children had their egg rolling, the Congressmen had their grass, and the White House had the start of a tradition.

THE CHILL IS GONE

This is not a very important fact unless you happen to be a President. Central heating was installed in the White House during **Franklin Pierce's** administration, in 1853.

CLEAN-UP WEEK

A man of taste, **Chester A. Arthur** refused to move into the White House in 1881 until the 81-year accumulation of its shabbier furniture and ornaments was removed.

They were.

There were 24 wagonfuls.

These were sold at auction. President Arthur had the interior redecorated and furnished by Louis Tiffany, and moved in.

MEMO

FROM: Warren G. Harding, President of the United States

TO: White House Staff

SUBJECT: Toothpicks

Please see that these are placed on all the tables.

WGH

Tidbits & Trivia

HOW DO YOU ADDRESS A LETTER TO THE PRESIDENT OF THE UNITED STATES IF YOU WISH TO USE THE CORRECT FORM, EVEN THOUGH YOU KNOW IT IS EXTREMELY UNLIKELY THAT YOU WILL RECEIVE AN ANSWER TO YOUR LETTER WRITTEN TO YOU BY THE PRESIDENT HIMSELF?

Dear Mr. President:

THE BEST REASON

Thomas Jefferson was reluctant to assume the responsibility for writing the Declaration of Independence, feeling that **John Adams** was better qualified. Conversely Adams thought Jefferson should be the author and told him why:

"Reason first: You are a Virginian, and Virginia ought to appear at the head of this business.

"Reason second: I am obnoxious, suspected and unpopular; you are very much otherwise.

"Reason third: You can write 10 times better than I can."

PRESIDENTS ON THE PRESIDENCY

I have had enough of it, heaven knows! I have had all the honor there is in this place, and have had responsibilities enough to kill any man.

William McKinley

YOUNG AT HEART

One President with the image of a bluff and hearty outdoorsman perhaps surprisingly could often be found playing games with children. On one occasion, **Theodore Roosevelt** exuberantly greeted his daughter and her chums with the suggestion, "Children, come with me — I'll teach you how to walk on stilts!"

One of T.R.'s best friends said, "One thing you must always remember about Roosevelt is that he is about seven years old."

PERMISSIVE PRESIDENTIAL PARENT

Theodore Roosevelt was a permissive father. One of the few recorded instances of his parental ire being roused resulted from an activity indulged in by his son Quentin. Since the family were residents of the White House, family members should, by all means, consider it their home. But one does not . . . repeat, DOES NOT . . . throw spitballs at the portrait of Andrew Jackson.

THE PRESIDENTS IN FOCUS

William Taft filled the camera's viewing frame completely.

Photographers and box cameras close in on Calvin Coolidge.

Early Years

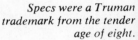

Specs were a Truman trademark from the tender age of eight.

Lyndon Johnson, "hunkered down" at age of 18 months.

John Kennedy, in need of knee patches at Dexter School.

Richard Nixon, not second fiddle for long.

Franklin Roosevelt was always close to his mother, Sara Delano.

The Eisenhower gene pool and some proud parents in 1902; Ike, extreme left, Milton — with curls, center front.

Those All-American Boys

Jerry Ford, lineperson for the University of Michigan football team, won three varsity letters.

Wide World

Wide World

Young Dwight Eisenhower boots one at a West Point football practice.

Franklin D. Roosevelt Library

Franklin Roosevelt (front row, second from left) did not win a football letter at Groton School.

Wide World

Dick Nixon (center) was known as "the most spirited bench warmer" at Whittier College.

Stout-hearted Men

Rancher Teddy Roosevelt
in 1883.

Mining engineer Herbert
Hoover in 1898.

Midshipman Jimmy
Carter in 1946.

In 1928 one out of four teachers
in Cotulla, Texas, dreamed of
becoming President of U.S.

Ass't Secretary of the Navy
F.D. Roosevelt on dry land.

Captain Harry Truman
in France in 1918.

Your friendly park ranger,
Gerald Ford, summer of '36.

We're Family

*Theodore and Edith Roosevelt and the kids
(Alice in white hat) at Oyster Bay.
Above: Sagamore Hill House in 1905.*

*Handsome couple and guard,
vital to 1953 Newport wedding.*

*President and Mrs. Woodrow Wilson married off two daughters
in the White House. This is Jessie's moment to glow*

*One of those "dog days" for F.D.R. and his family at
Campobello in 1920; only "Chief" seems to be enjoying it.
Right: Roosevelt Hyde Park mansion.*

At Ease

Nixon being driven to another crisis.

Calvin Coolidge always wore something comfortable when relaxing on his Vermont farm.

Ike was serious about his painting.

"Fala" and friend enjoying a country drive.

Reagan getting on his high horse at the ranch in California.

Hoover was serious about his fishing — hence hat, coat, and tie.

Carter batting stance shows keen eye for high, fast balls.

132 Rms
Riv vu

The high point of summer in Washington once was watching the cows cooling off at the river. This was the frantic pace in 1882.

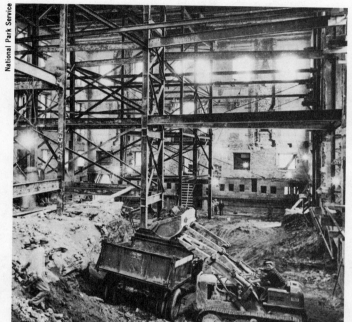

The Truman bare-walls redo of the White House came about when someone noticed the sag under Harry's piano.

Mrs. Benjamin Harrison's plan to enlarge the White House would impress any imperial-minded Chief Executive. Congress did not approve.

Sheep grazing on the White House grounds, part of Wilson's wartime economies.

The East Room of the White House in its "steamboat Gothic" decor of 1893.

A four-man tub made to order for President Taft.

Ceremonial
Chores

Morning roll call of the White House guards includes two Theodore Roosevelt offspring, Archie and Quentin.

Changing of the Nixon guard at the White House in 1970. The show closed after only a few performances.

The Grants drop in at a Nevada mine, 1879. Julia (third from left) did not want to go down the mine, but changed her mind upon hearing that her husband had bet on her not going.

Gerald Ford clogging it at festival in Holland, Michigan.

Teddy Roosevelt gets to run a steam shovel in Panama.

Big Bill Taft and other top-hatted dignitaries find their tour of the Panama Canal lacks motive power.

"Chief" Roosevelt and Indian-giver at Boy Scout camp in 1933.

An American sailor receives a medal from Cal Coolidge.

An American general receives a medal from Harry Truman.

The Monument Works

Putting in the final pieces at Lincoln Memorial. Sculptor Daniel Chester French (foreground), doubled the final size of the statue for effect.

Visitors and attendants at temporary vault for General Grant, New York, ca. 1885.

Grant's Tomb as it looks today.

Gothic tracery is the motif on enclosure for Monroe's tomb in Richmond.

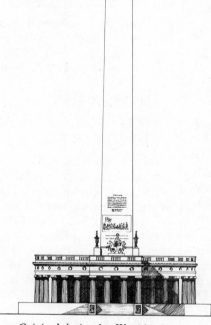

Original design for Washington Monument included an elaborate base, a case where more was less.

Putting the last jackhammer touches to Lincoln's face on Mt. Rushmore, 1940.

John F. Kennedy Library, rejected by Cambridge, got a Boston Harbor view at the Dorchester Bay site.

Lots of glass in the attractive Gerald R. Ford Museum, in Ann Arbor, Michigan.

Lyndon B. Johnson Library and Museum, like the man, looms tall in Austin, Texas.

THE PRESIDENTS

THE FIRST

The first President to have an automobile at the White House was **William Howard Taft,** in 1909. Actually he had four, a White Steamer, a Baker Electric, and two Pierce Arrows.

The first President to ride to his inauguration in an automobile was **Warren Harding,** in 1921.

WHAT'S BETTER THAN VICE?

Eight men who first held the office of Vice-President of the United States later ran for the presidency and were elected to the highest office. The men:

John Adams, Thomas Jefferson, Martin Van Buren, Theodore Roosevelt, Calvin Coolidge, Harry Truman, Lyndon Johnson, and **Richard Nixon.**

A STAR IS BORN

The first President to have starred in a Hollywood movie was **Ronald Reagan.** He appeared in more than 50 films and was the host for two dramatic television series.

VALOR

Two sons of Presidents were awarded the Congressional Medal of Honor.

Rutherford B. Hayes' son Webb received the medal for his actions on December 4, 1899, in the Philippine campaign of the Spanish-American War.

Theodore Roosevelt's son, Theodore Roosevelt, Jr., was awarded the medal for his performance in Normandy on June 6, 1944, D-Day.

A REAL STATESMAN

Benjamin Harrison's administration saw more states admitted to the Union than any other. They were the thirty-ninth through the forty-fourth: North Dakota, South Dakota, Montana, Washington, Idaho and Wyoming.

IF IT DOESN'T FIT, YOU CAN ALWAYS RETURN IT

On May 29, 1938, his 21st birthday, **John F. Kennedy** received a very nice birthday gift from his father, a $1,000,000 trust fund.

CHECK THOSE RATINGS!

Franklin D. Roosevelt was the first presidential TV star, appearing on NBC April 30, 1939, at the opening of the World's Fair.

TRUMAN ON TRAINS: THE ONLY WAY TO FLY

Harry S Truman never was convinced that old-fashioned whistle-stop campaigning was passé even when air travel became the order of the day. He told **LBJ,** then running for election, "You may not believe this, Lyndon, but there are still a hell of a lot of people in this country who don't know where the airport is. But they damn sure know where the depot is. And if you let 'em know you're coming, they'll be down and listen to you."

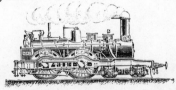

LOOKING BACK

In retirement, former President **Harry S Truman** observed that "Three things can ruin a man — money, power and women. I never had any money, I never wanted power, and the only woman in my life is up at the house right now."

S FOR BOTH

Harry Truman's paternal grandfather's name began with an S. Harry Truman's maternal grandfather's name began with an S. In order to honor both and offend neither, Harry Truman was given a middle name that began with an S . . . and stopped right there.

Tidbits & Trivia

THE ADAMS FAMILY HEIRLOOMS STRIKE AGAIN

A visit from First Lady Lady Bird Johnson to the Adams homestead in Quincy, Massachusetts, brought eight Adams kin together in the Old House for a glass of sherry while the current First Lady met the descendants of the second.

Abigail Adams Homans, at 88 the patrician family's matriarch, deep in conversation with Lady Bird, gestured with her wineglass, which shattered against a piece of furniture.

"Hell," Mrs. Homans exclaimed. "I do hope that wasn't one of the historic ones."

THESE THINGS TAKE TIME

Shortly after he became President, **Gerald Ford** had a visitor. The visitor looked around the room. There was a large painting hanging on the wall. The visitor studied the painting.

"Is that a Gilbert Stuart?" he asked the President.

"I don't know," replied Ford. "I haven't been here long enough."

NO INSOMNIAC HE

William Howard Taft was a man who fell asleep. He could fall asleep any time, anywhere. He was brilliant at it. Probably his outstanding achievement in this respect was the time he fell asleep at a funeral.

MRS. PRESIDENT

Edith Wilson, the second wife of **Woodrow Wilson,** may have been the most controversial First Lady of all, for when her husband was stricken with a serious stroke, she decided that he could "still do more with a maimed body than anyone else," and everyone who wanted to see him had to come through her, while she determined which matters were important enough for his attention.

She called it her "Stewardship," but others referred to the period as "Mrs. Wilson's Regency," and labelled her "Mrs. President."

The President's doctors upheld her, however, and insisted that any attempt to declare Wilson incompetent would fail, for they agreed with Edith that his mind was "clear as crystal."

In the face of criticism, Edith maintained that, "I, myself, never made a single decision regarding the disposition of public affairs." Whatever decisions she made must have been good ones, however, for

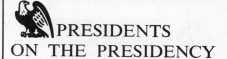

PRESIDENTS ON THE PRESIDENCY

"I'm like the man who was tarred and feathered and ridden out of town on a rail. When they asked him how he felt about it, he said that if it weren't for the honor of the thing, he would rather have walked."

Abraham Lincoln

it was not until nearly half a century later, in 1967, that the twenty-fifth Amendment to the Constitution, "Presidential Disability and Succession," was passed.

THE PRESIDENTS

MS. PRES

Hannah Van Buren

Letitia Tyler

Eliza Johnson

Wives of the Presidents	Born	Married	Died	Age	Sons	Daughters
Martha Dandridge [Custis] Washington[1]	1731	1759	1802	70	two[2]	two[2]
Abigail Smith Adams	1744	1764	1818	73	three	two
Martha Wayles [Skelton] Jefferson[3]	1748	1772	1782	33	two[4]	five
Dolley Payne [Todd] Madison[5]	1768	1794	1849	81	two[2]	....
Elizabeth Kortright Monroe	1768	1786	1830	62	one	two
Louisa Catherine Johnson Adams	1775	1797	1852	77	three	one
Rachel Donelson [Robards] Jackson[6]	1767	1791	1828	61	....	....
Hannah Hoes Van Buren	1783	1807	1819	35	four	....
Anna Symmes Harrison	1775	1795	1864	88	six	four
Letitia Christian Tyler	1790	1813	1842	51	three	five
Julia Gardiner Tyler	1820	1844	1889	69	five	two
Sarah Childress Polk	1803	1824	1891	87	....	....
Margaret Smith Taylor	1788	1810	1852	63	one	five
Abigail Powers Fillmore	1798	1826	1853	55	one	one
Caroline Carmichael [McIntosh] Fillmore[7]	1813	1858	1881	67	....	....
Jane Appleton Pierce	1806	1834	1863	57	three	....
Mary Todd Lincoln	1818	1842	1882	63	four	....
Eliza McCardle Johnson	1810	1827	1876	65	three	two
Julia Dent Grant	1826	1848	1902	76	three	one
Lucy Webb Hayes	1831	1852	1889	57	seven	one
Lucretia Rudolph Garfield	1832	1858	1918	85	five	two
Ellen Herndon Arthur	1837	1859	1880	42	two	one
Frances Folsom Cleveland[8]	1864	1886	1947	83	two	three
Caroline Scott Harrison	1832	1853	1892	60	one	one
Mary Lord [Dimmick] Harrison[9]	1858	1896	1948	89	....	one

[1] Widow of Colonel Daniel Parke Custis
[2] Children from first marriage
[3] Widow of Bathurst Skelton
[4] One son from first marriage
[5] Widow of John Todd, Sr.
[6] Divorcee of Captain Lewis Robards
[7] Widow of Ezekiel C. McIntosh
[8] Remarried in 1913 to Thomas J. Preston, Jr.
[9] Widow of Walter Erskine Dimmick

Tidbits & Trivia

Wives of the Presidents	Born	Married	Died	Age	Sons	Daughters
Ida Saxton McKinley	1847	1871	1907	59	....	two
Alice Lee Roosevelt	1861	1880	1884	22	....	one
Edith Carow Roosevelt	1861	1886	1948	87	four	one
Helen Herron Taft	1861	1886	1943	82	two	one
Ellen Axson Wilson	1860	1885	1914	54	....	three
Edith Bolling [Galt] Wilson[1]	1872	1915	1961	89	....	....
Florence Kling [De Wolfe] Harding[2]	1860	1891	1924	64	one[3]	....
Grace Goodhue Coolidge	1879	1905	1957	78	two	....
Lou Henry Hoover	1875	1899	1944	68	two	....
Anna Eleanor Roosevelt	1884	1905	1962	78	five	one
Elizabeth Wallace Truman	1885	1919	....	....	....	one
Mary (Mamie) Doud Eisenhower	1896	1916	1979	82	two	....
Jacqueline Bouvier Kennedy[4]	1929	1953	....	....	two	one
Claudia (Lady Bird) Taylor Johnson	1912	1934	....	....	....	two
Thelma (Patricia) Ryan Nixon	1912	1940	....	....	....	two
Elizabeth Bloomer [Warren] Ford[5]	1918	1948	....	....	three	one
Rosalynn Smith Carter	1927	1946	....	....	three	one

[1] Widow of Norman Galt
[2] Divorcee of Henry De Wolfe
[3] Child from first marriage
[4] Remarried in 1968 to Aristotle Onassis
[5] Divorcee of William Warren

Frances Cleveland

Florence Harding

THE BEAUTIFUL PEOPLE

A very tired newswoman, having dogged Lady Bird Johnson's footsteps all across the country and back on her Beautification projects, pointed out that "It's Lady Bird's traveling companions, not the places they visit, who need preservation and beautification on one of her trips."

DAUGHTERLY ADVICE

Asked for advice for young people whose fathers might aspire to the presidency, Lynda Johnson said, "Don't encourage him."

RIGHT ON, ABIGAIL

A woman ahead of her time, Abigail Adams fired off this letter to her husband, John. The year: 1774.

"Whilst you are proclaiming peace and good-will to men, emancipating all nations, you insist on retaining absolute power over wives . . . Remember the ladies and be more generous and favorable to them than your ancestors . . . Do not put such unlimited power into the hands of the husbands . . . If particular care and attention is not paid to the ladies, we are deter-

mined to foment a rebellion and will not hold ourselves bound by any laws in which we have no voice or representation."

THE PRESIDENTS

NEPOTISM STRIKES AGAIN

Andrew Jackson had no children of his own he could install in the White House, but he did have a niece. Maybe he couldn't make her President, but he could make her First Lady. So he told Sarah Childress, "Daughter, I will put you in the White House if it costs me my life."

Her husband was **James K. Polk.**

THEY JUST WANTED TO BE SURE

Bess Wallace was **Harry Truman's** childhood sweetheart. He first met her when he was six and she was five.

And so they were married . . . nearly 30 years later, when the persistent beau was 35 and his bride was 34.

That's not exactly giving 'em hell, Harry.

GONE FISHIN'

A number of Presidents were enthusiastic fishermen. One of them was **Benjamin Harrison,** a somewhat formal and formidable gentleman, but apparently not when he went on a fishing trip. According to an old friend of Ben's who went fishing with him often, "When he's on a fishing trip, Ben takes his drink of whiskey in the morning, just like anyone else. He chews tobacco from a plug he carries in his hip pocket, spits on his worm for luck, and cusses when the fish gets away."

THERE'S NO ROOM HERE FOR THE BOTH OF US

Although hesitant to move his army against that of Robert E. Lee, General George McClellan was not in the least reluctant to give **Abraham Lincoln** advice about how to run the country.

When someone asked Lincoln if he was going to do anything about it, the President replied that, no, he wasn't. McClellan, he commented, reminded him of a man who was riding his horse one day, when the horse kicked and got its foot caught in one of the stirrups.

"Hold on there," said the man to the horse. "If you're gonna get on, I'm getting off."

THERE ONCE WAS A FELLOW NAMED WOODROW . . .

President **Woodrow Wilson,** despite his severe demeanor, was a man in whom a spring of humor bubbled. He enjoyed a good story and could tell one. He also liked limericks. This was one of his favorites:

For beauty I am not a star.
There are others more handsome by far.
But my face, I don't mind it
Because I'm behind it.
It's the people in front whom I jar.

TOUGH ACT TO FOLLOW

President **James Garfield** had a trick. It was a very good trick. It took him four years of college to learn it. A classics man, Garfield was able to, and did when asked, simultaneously write Greek with one hand and Latin with the other.

Tidbits & Trivia

ABE LINCOLN, A DAY IN THE LIFE OF

We are all subjected to a steady stream of media trivia about our Presidents, the details of their private lives, their families, relatives, pets, ad infinitum, from the time they take office until a new President is elected. Sometimes the sum total of the observations is greater than the parts, as in this account of **Lincoln** in the White House by John Hay, one of Lincoln's private secretaries.

"Lincoln used to go to bed ordinarily from ten to eleven o'clock unless he happened to be kept up by important news, in which case he would frequently remain at the War Department till one or two. He rose early. When he lived in the country at the Soldiers' Home, he would be up and dressed, eat his breakfast (which was extremely frugal, an egg, a piece of toast, coffee, etc.), and ride into Washington, all before eight o'clock. In the winter at the White House he was not quite so early. He did not sleep well, but spent a good while in bed. Tad (his son) usually slept with him. He would lie

around the office until he fell asleep and Lincoln would shoulder him and take him off to bed. He pretended to begin business at ten o'clock in the morning, but in reality the ante-rooms and halls were full before that hour — people anxious to get the first axe ground.

"He was extremely unmethodical: it was a four years' struggle on Nicolay's part and mine to get him to adopt some systematic rules. He would break through every regulation as fast as it was made. Anything that kept the people themselves away from him he disapproved, although they nearly annoyed the life out of him by unreasonable complaints and requests . . . .

"The House remained full of people nearly all day. At noon the President took a little lunch — a biscuit, a glass of milk in winter, some fruit or grapes in summer. He dined between five and six, and we went off to our dinner also. Before dinner was over, members and Senators would come back and take up the whole evening. Sometimes, though rarely, he shut himself up and would see no one. Sometimes he would run away to a lecture or concert or theater for the sake of a little rest. He was very abstemious — ate less than anyone I know. He drank nothing but water, not from principle but because he did not like wine or spirits."

ZERO PROOF

Mrs. Rutherford B. Hayes was known as "Lemonade Lucy," for she permitted no beverage stronger than that to be served at White House functions.

A guest, describing one such affair, remarked, "The water flowed like wine."

A MATTER OF INTERPRETATION

Some historians say that **Franklin Pierce** was an alcoholic.

Other historians say that Franklin Pierce was a reformed alcoholic.

Some historians are kinder than other historians.

THE PRESIDENTS

LINCOLN SPOKE HERE

The political destiny of **Abraham Lincoln** is thought by many to have begun at Springfield, Ill., on June 16, 1858, when he delivered the "house divided" speech to open his campaign for Stephen Douglas's seat in the U.S. Senate. A month later he challenged Douglas to a series of debates which carried the two men across the state and Lincoln to national prominence. (Douglas was reelected to his Senate seat, for the Democrats still controlled the state assembly, but Lincoln polled a popular majority.)

Afterward Lincoln was deluged with requests to speak in a number of places. He responded to the appeals and began touring the country, speaking to crowds in the midwest, New York, and New England. Lincoln's public career and his rise to greatness can be charted by noting the places where he addressed the people of this nation. The list of sites and towns is longer than one might think and includes many besides those in Lincoln country.

New Salem, Ill.	March 9, 1831	First political speech
New Salem, Ill.	March 9, 1832	Announced candidacy for State Legislature
Vandalia, Ill.	December 1834	On taking seat in State Legislature
New Salem, Ill.	July-August 1836	Campaign speeches for reelection
Springfield, Ill.	January 27, 1838	Lyceum speech on national survival
Vandalia, Ill.	December 20, 1839	First major speech in State Legislature
Springfield, Ill.	June 18, 1840	First argument before Illinois Supreme Court
Springfield, Ill.	February 22, 1842	Spoke before temperance society
Vincennes and Rockport, Ind.	October 1844	Speeches in support of presidential candidate Henry Clay
Bruceville, Ind.	October 26, 1844	Spoke on visit to boyhood home
Springfield, Ill.	July 31, 1846	Address on his religious convictions
Oregon, Ill.	August 16, 1846	Spoke after election to U.S. Congress
Springfield, Ill.	May 16, 1847	Addressed temperance society
Washington, D.C.	January 12, 1848	Spoke in Congress on "spot resolutions"
Washington, D.C.	June 20, 1848	Spoke in Congress on internal improvements
Washington, D.C.	July 27, 1848	Spoke in Congress on qualifications of Gen. Taylor for President
Worcester, Mass.	September 12, 1848	Speech advocating Taylor for President
Boston, Mass.	September 15, 1848	Speech for Taylor
Chicago, Ill.	October 6, 1848	Addressed Whig rally
Springfield, Ill.	July 25, 1850	Delivered eulogy on Zachary Taylor
Springfield, Ill.	July 16, 1852	Delivered eulogy on Henry Clay
Springfield, Ill.	June 14, 1854	Introduced former President Millard Fillmore
Springfield, Ill.	September 4, 1854	Announced candidacy for State Legislature
Peoria, Ill.	October 16, 1854	Spoke on repeal of Missouri Compromise
Decatur, Ill.	February 22, 1856	Important speech before Editor's Convention
Bloomington, Ill.	May 29, 1856	Delivered "lost speech"
Chicago, Ill.	July 19, 1856	Delivered campaign speech for Frémont
Galena, Ill.	July 23, 1856	Campaign speech for Frémont
Chicago, Ill.	December 10, 1856	Spoke at Republican banquet
Springfield, Ill.	June 26, 1857	Speech on Dred Scott decision
Springfield, Ill.	June 16, 1858	Delivered "house divided" speech to open campaign for U.S. Senate
Chicago, Ill.	July 10, 1858	Spoke on popular sovereignty
Sterling, Ill.	July 15, 1858	Addressed Republican rally
Springfield, Ill.	July 17, 1858	Speech on Dred Scott decision
Clinton, Ill.	July 27, 1858	Speech on "fooling the people"
Havanna, Ill.	August 14, 1858	Reply to earlier Douglas speech
Ottawa, Ill.	August 21, 1858	First debate with Douglas
Amboy, Ill.	August 26, 1858	Short address
Freeport, Ill.	August 27, 1858	Second debate with Douglas
Carlinville, Ill.	August 31, 1858	Short address
Paris, Ill.	September 8, 1858	Speech on popular sovereignty
Edwardsville, Ill.	September 10, 11, 1858	Campaign speeches
Jonesboro, Ill.	September 15, 1858	Third debate with Douglas
Charleston, Ill.	September 18, 1858	Fourth debate with Douglas
Danville, Ill.	September 21, 1858	Short address
Galesburg, Ill.	October 7, 1858	Fifth debate with Douglas
Quincy, Ill.	October 13, 1858	Sixth debate with Douglas

Tidbits & Trivia

Alton, Ill.	October 15, 1858	Seventh and last debate with Douglas
Rushville, Ill.	October 20, 1858	Campaign speech
Carthage, Ill.	October 22, 1858	Spoke before 2,000 women
Jacksonville, Ill.	February 11, 1859	Lecture on discoveries and inventions
Chicago, Ill.	March 1; 1859	Speech before Republican rally
Council Bluffs, Iowa	August 13, 1859	Address while on midwest tour to gain recognition as presidential candidate
Columbus, Ohio	September 16, 1859	Spoke for Republican state ticket
Cincinnati, Ohio	September 17, 1859	Continued arguments begun at Columbus
Dayton, Ohio	September 17, 1859	Delivered address
Hamilton, Ohio	September 17, 1859	Delivered address
Indianapolis, Ind.	September 19, 1859	Delivered address
Milwaukee, Wis.	September 30, 1859	Spoke on agriculture
Troy and Doniphan, Kans.	December 1, 1859	Short speeches on Kansas tour
Atchison, Kans.	December 2, 1859	Speech on Kansas tour
Leavenworth, Kans.	December 3, 1859	Speech on Kansas tour
New York, N.Y.	February 27, 1860	Cooper Institute address
Providence, R.I.	March 1, 1860	First speech on New England tour as presidential candidate
Dover, N.H.	March 2, 1860	Campaign speech
Concord, Mass.	March 3, 1860	Campaign speech
Manchester, Mass.	March 3, 1860	Campaign speech
Hartford, Conn.	March 5, 1860	Speech on slavery issue
New Haven, Conn.	March 6, 1860	Campaign speech
Meridian, Conn. and Woonsocket, R.I.	March 8, 1860	Campaign speeches
Waukegan, Ill.	April 2, 1860	Campaign speech
Decatur, Ill.	May 9, 1860	Speech after nomination as Illinois "favorite son"
Springfield, Ill.	August 8, 1860	Speech to friends and neighbors as Republican nominee for President
Springfield, Ill.	February 11, 1861	Farewell address to Springfield
Tolono, Ill.	February 11, 1861	Short address from train on leaving Illinois
Indianapolis, Ill.	February 12, 1861	Speech en route to Washington
Columbus, Ohio	February 13, 1861	Speech to Ohio Legislature
Steubenville, Ohio	February 14, 1861	Speech
Pittsburgh, Pa.	February 15, 1861	Speech
Cleveland, Ohio	February 15, 1861	Speech
Buffalo, N.Y.	February 16, 1861	Speech
Rochester, N.Y.	February 18, 1861	Speech
Utica, N.Y.	February 18, 1861	Speech
Albany, N.Y.	February 18, 1861	Speech
Troy, N.Y.	February 19, 1861	Speech
Hudson, N.Y.	February 19, 1861	Speech
Poughkeepsie, N.Y.	February 19, 1861	Speech
New York, N.Y.	February 19, 20, 1861	Two speeches
Trenton, N.J.	February 21, 1861	Speech to N.J. Assembly
Philadelphia, Pa.	February 22, 1861	Speech at Independence Hall
Harrisburg, Pa.	February 22, 1861	Speech to Pennsylvania Legislature
Washington, D.C.	March 4, 1861	Inaugural address
Washington, D.C.	August 6, 1861	Spoke on war effort
Frederick, Md.	October 4, 1862	Spoke after visit to Antietam battlefield
Gettysburg, Pa.	November 19, 1863	Delivered Gettysburg Address
Washington, D.C.	August 18, 1864	Address to 164th Ohio Regiment
Washington, D.C.	August 31, 1864	Address to 148th Ohio Regiment
Princeton, N.J.	December 20, 1864	Remarks after receiving honorary degree from Princeton
Washington, D.C.	March 4, 1865	Second inaugural address
Richmond, Va.	April 4, 1865	Brief remarks on visit to fallen city
Washington, D.C.	April 10, 1865	Remarks to crowd on news of end of war
Washington, D.C.	April 11, 1865	Speech on reconstruction (last public speech)

THE PRESIDENTS

THAT DOG IN THE WHITE HOUSE

The most famous dog ever to be an occupant of the White House was **Franklin Roosevelt's** Scottie, Fala. They were inseparable companions.

In the summer of 1944, Fala accompanied his master on a voyage to Hawaii aboard the cruiser *Baltimore*. Fala, no longer young, was causing some concern. He kept disappearing for hours at a time, which was not like him, and the President also noticed that the dog's hair seemed to be falling out.

Upon investigation, the disappearances and the falling hair proved to be closely connected. Some of the crew members had been enticing Fala to their dining quarters by feeding him tidbits. On those occasions the sailors snipped off locks of his coat for souvenirs. When the President found out, both feeding and snipping stopped short.

That fall, Roosevelt, campaigning for his fourth term, made one of the most memorable and successful political speeches of all time. The most memorable part of the speech was devoted to friend Fala. "These Republican leaders," said FDR, "have not been content with attacks on me, or my wife, or on my sons. No, not content with that, they now include my little dog, Fala. Well, of course, I don't resent attacks, and my family doesn't resent attacks but Fala *does* resent them. You know, Fala is Scotch, and being a Scottie, as soon as he learned that the Republican fiction writers in Congress and out, had concocted a story that I had left him behind on the Aleutian Islands and had sent a destroyer back to find him — at a cost to the taxpayers of two or three, or eight or twenty million dollars — his Scotch soul was furious. He has not been the same since. I am accustomed to hearing malicious falsehoods about myself — such as that old worm-eaten chestnut that I have represented myself as indispensible. But I think I have the right to resent, to object to libelous statements about my dog."

FOR OPENERS

Among the more personally revealing statements made by a candidate for the presidency was that given by **Warren Harding.** Upon being informed that his party had nominated him for the highest office in the land, Harding offered this statesmanlike utterance:

"We drew to a pair of deuces and filled."

WITH FRIENDS LIKE THAT . . .

Warren Harding was a man who trusted the friends he'd appointed to key positions in his administration. He shouldn't have, and he knew it, but only after the lid was off their Teapot Dome scandal and the corruption had boiled over.

"In this job I'm not worried about my enemies," said the disillusioned Harding. "It's my friends, my Goddamn friends, who are keeping me awake nights."

WHO, ME?

Harry Truman, learning he had unexpectedly been tapped for the vice-presidency by **FDR,** said "Why, I've hardly been to the White House!"

ONLY ONE . . .

Only one President was awarded a Pulitzer Prize. Author of *Profiles in Courage,* **John F. Kennedy** received the prize for biography.

PROFOUND, PROFOUND!

Calvin Coolidge said it. "When more and more people are thrown out of work, unemployment results."

Tidbits & Trivia

ONLY ONE...

Dwight Eisenhower was the only President to hold a pilot's license.

PRAISE FROM THE MAN FROM MISSOURI

Harry Truman admired **John Adams'** wife, Abigail. An avid reader of history, the well-informed Harry said of her, "Abigail would have made a better President than her husband."

Or maybe Harry just didn't like John.

A FUTURE PRESIDENT'S BEST FRIEND IS HIS MOTHER

Harry Truman claimed his mother had started it all when she bought her young son a blackboard with the Presidents' biographies on it. He said he learned to "think President" then, but by the time it actually happened to him, he was "certainly not thinking of that blackboard anymore."

MARTHA GETS TOP BILLING

The first bill bearing the portrait of a woman was the one-dollar silver certificate issued in September 1886. Who was that Lady? Martha Washington.

PERSONAL PRIVILEGE

Three Presidents, **Thomas Jefferson, Abraham Lincoln,** and **Andrew Johnson,** had no formal religious affiliation.

NOBEL PEACE PRIZE

The Nobel Peace Prize was awarded to two Presidents. In 1906 it was awarded to **Theodore Roosevelt** for his service in ending the Russo-Japanese War. In 1919 it went to **Woodrow Wilson** for his efforts in creating the League of Nations following World War I.

YOU CAN'T HAVE EVERYTHING

In 1892, **Grover Cleveland** ran against Benjamin Harrison in a truly "so what?" campaign. Support for both men was somewhat less than unenthusiastic. The whole thing was aptly described by an observer who said, "Each side would have been glad to defeat the other if it could do so without electing its own candidate."

Once in a while there are years like that.

FIRST DAUGHTERS ON THE WHITE HOUSE

Margaret Truman called it "The Great White Jail." Lynda and Luci Johnson thought it even worse than that. They said it was "A Great White Mausoleum."

THE PRESIDENTS

THE FIRST

Franklin Roosevelt was the first Chief Executive whose mother could, and presumably did, vote for her son for President.

GREAT OAKS... AND ETC.

Following his graduation from Harvard at the age of 20, **John Adams** became a grammar-school master in Worcester, Massachusetts.

"My little school," he commented, "like the great world, is made up of Kings, politicians, divines, fops, buffoons, fiddlers, fools, coxcombs, sycophants, chimney sweeps, and every other character I see in the world. I would rather sit in school and consider which of my pupils will turn out to be a hero, and which a rake, which a philosopher and which a parasite, than to have an income of a thousand pounds a year." He made no mention of what he thought the teacher might become.

NO FAITH

"An atheist," said **Dwight D. Eisenhower,** "is a guy who watches a Notre Dame-SMU football game and doesn't care who wins."

SPORTING LIFE

One of the White House's greatest athletes was **Jerry Ford,** a former football hero who endured good-naturedly countless jokes about his so-called clumsiness, slow mental processes due to "having been hit too many times with his helmet off," and Lyndon Johnson's memorable quip that "the trouble with Jerry Ford is he couldn't walk and chew gum at the same time."

Instead of annoying Ford, the jokes seemed to delight him. He began telling them on himself.

About his golf game: "I have a very wild swing. I'll tell you how wild it is. Back on my home course in Michigan, they don't yell 'Fore!' they yell, 'Ford!'

"In Washington, I'm known as President of the United States, but in golf, I'm known as the 'jinx of the links.'"

MADAME LAFAYETTE, WE ARE HERE

The year: 1796. The place: Le Plessis Prison, Paris. Adrienne, wife of the Marquis de Lafayette, had been imprisoned there during the French Revolution and was awaiting the guillotine. Her mother and grandmother had met that fate.

A carriage drew up to the prison gate. Madame Lafayette had a visitor. A crowd gathered. Who was the visitor speaking to Madame Lafayette by the prison gate? She seemed a lady of importance, and she was.

Mrs. James Monroe, wife of the American Minister to France, had come at her husband's request to demonstrate publicly America's sympathy for the prisoner, which his own position officially precluded him from doing.

Madame Lafayette was deeply affected. When they found out who

the visitor was, the crowd, too, was deeply affected. News of the visit soon spread throughout the city.

Monroe had hoped that the visit might create public sympathy for the prisoner and that public opinion might sway the authorities to release her. It did.

Shortly after, as a direct result of Elizabeth Monroe's visit, Adrienne Lafayette was granted her freedom.

Tidbits & Trivia

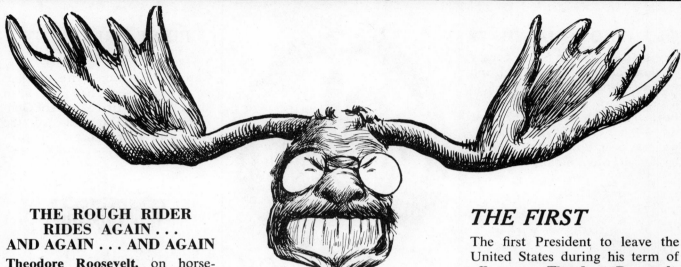

THE ROUGH RIDER RIDES AGAIN... AND AGAIN... AND AGAIN

Theodore Roosevelt, on horseback, led his Rough Riders in their charge up San Juan Hill during the Spanish-American War.

Changing only his mode of transportation, T.R. continued to maintain his position at the front of the group. He was the first President to:

Ride in an automobile, 1902.

Submerge in a submarine, 1905.

Fly in an airplane, 1910 (as ex-President).

Land. Sea. Air. That seems to about cover it, Teddy.

PISTOL PACKIN' PRES.

Following the assassination of William McKinley, President **Teddy Roosevelt** took to carrying a gun in public so he would "have some chance of shooting the assassin before he could shoot me."

THE FIRST

The first President to leave the United States during his term of office was **Theodore Roosevelt,** who went to Panama in November 1906 aboard the battleship USS *Louisiana* to inspect the progress being made on the Panama Canal.

THE PRESIDENTS

OLD WHO AND WHAT?

During the Mexican War **Zachary Taylor,** known as "Old Rough and Ready," and General Winfield Scott, known as "Old Fuss and Feathers," both were on the same side — our side. By the time the war was over, both had won major battles and were national heroes.

As a result, the two generals now took opposite sides, each seeking the presidential nomination at the Whig Party convention.

In the Battle of the Whig Convention, Old Rough and Ready defeated Old Fuss and Feathers.

It sure has been a long time since candidates had names like that.

A STAR IS BORN

Asked if he knew General Douglas MacArthur well, **Dwight Eisenhower** replied, "Yes, I know him well. Very well indeed. I studied dramatics under him for years."

FIRST PRESIDENT GENERAL

Caroline Harrison, wife of Benjamin Harrison, had her own army. She was first President General of the Daughters of the American Revolution.

18, 19, 20

The eighteenth President of the United States was **Ulysses S. Grant.** He was born in Ohio. He was a general in the Civil War.

The nineteenth President of the United States was **Rutherford B. Hayes.** He was born in Ohio. He was a general in the Civil War.

The twentieth President of the United States was **James A. Garfield.** He was born in Ohio. He was a general in the Civil War.

18, 19, 20. A trifecta.

DO YOU GET A PURPLE HEART FOR THAT?

Franklin Pierce served as a brigadier general in the Mexican War, but not for long.

There he was, sitting on his horse at the start of his first battle. The horse didn't like the battle. It didn't like the noise. It didn't like the artillery shells bursting all around. The horse panicked. When it panicked, it bucked. When it bucked, it threw Franklin Pierce forward against the pommel of the saddle. It threw him against the pommel hard. Ouch, that smarts!

Then to add injury to injury, the horse fell on Pierce, wrenching the General's knee. Only after he finished noticing the first injury did he become aware of the injury to his knee when he found that he couldn't walk.

Pierce stayed in Mexico only long enough to acquire a severe case of a local intestinal ailment known as Montezuma's Revenge.

During the mudslinging that went on during the presidential campaign of 1852, the unkindest cut made by the opposition was that Franklin Pierce had not conducted himself heroically in the Mexican War.

Tidbits & Trivia

TWO PRESIDENTS WERE SLAVES

Enslavement of blacks wasn't the only kind of slavery practiced in this country. The indentured servant was a different kind of slave, bound by a contract to work for a master who, in effect, owned him for the term of the contract.

As boys, Presidents **Millard Fillmore** and **Andrew Johnson** both had been indentured. They didn't like it.

Johnson, indentured to a tailor, ran away. The tailor took out an ad in the Raleigh, North Carolina, *Gazette,* offering a $10 reward for the return of the future President. There were no takers.

Fillmore, indentured to a clothmaker, served his master for several years and finally bought his freedom for $30.

Apparently Fillmore was worth $20 more than Andy Johnson.

ONLY A DREAM?

Julia Tyler had a terrible nightmare. She dreamed her husband, **John Tyler** was dying in Richmond, where he'd gone to attend the Confederate Congress. She rushed to his side, finding him perfectly well, having recovered from a slight indisposition he'd suffered a few days before.

Suddenly, two days later, he was dead. The Confederacy accorded him a hero's burial. The United States of America, however, for the first and only time in its history, completely ignored the death of a former President.

READING 'RITIN' AND ROMANCE

She was only a shoemaker's daughter, but Eliza McCardle was a bright lass who knew her ABC's. Just sixteen when she married **Andrew Johnson**, Eliza taught her tailor husband how to read and write while he stitched and stitched.

THE ROOKIE AND THE VETERAN

Andrew Johnson was 19 when he became a father for the first time.

John Tyler was 70 when he became a father for the last time.

And there are still some people who call baseball the American Pastime.

THE PRESIDENTS

A LITTLE ADVICE

Princess Margaret of Great Britain and her husband, Lord Snowden, were visiting the White House. President **Lyndon Johnson** took the occasion to give the Earl a piece of husbandly advice.

"I've learned that there are only two things necessary to keep your wife happy," said Lyndon. "First, let her think she's having her way. And second, let her have it."

NO RELATION

A lifelong Republican, Edith Roosevelt wanted to make one thing perfectly clear. **Franklin Roosevelt** was no kin to her. He was, she said, a "distant cousin of my husband."

THANKS TO HER IT'S WORKING

Lady Bird Johnson knew her Beautification Program was paying off when she read a cartoon featuring a billboard proclaiming: "Impeach Lady Bird."

She hopes her epitaph will read, "She planted a tree."

WHAT'S A MOTHER TO DO?

Edith Roosevelt was a patient women when it came to **Teddy Roosevelt's** foibles, and she was as energetic as he in pursuing the outdoor life. On at least one occasion, however, she admitted that being on call virtually 24 hours a day to comfort his regiment of Rough Riders had strained her good nature to its outer limits. Taking care of the Rough Riders, she said, was like being "parents to a thousand very large and very bad children."

She should know. She raised six herself.

English (15)

Washington
J. Adams
Madison
J. Q. Adams
W. H. Harrison
Tyler
Taylor
Fillmore
Pierce
Lincoln
B. Harrison
Coolidge
L. B. Johnson
Ford
Carter

English, Scots-Irish (8)

A. Johnson
Arthur
McKinley
Cleveland
Taft
Harding
Truman
Nixon

Scots-Irish (4)

Jackson
Polk
Buchanan
Wilson

PRESIDENTIAL ANCESTRY

Dutch (3)

Van Buren
T. Roosevelt
F. D. Roosevelt

English, Scottish (2)

Grant
Hayes

Swiss-German (2)

Hoover
Eisenhower

English, French (1)

Garfield

Irish (1)

Kennedy

Irish, Scottish, English (1)

Reagan

Scottish, Welsh (1)

Monroe

Welsh (1)

Jefferson

Tidbits & Trivia

PUT THEM ALL TOGETHER, THEY SPELL MOTHER

Virginia is a mother. She is known as the Mother of Presidents. Eight of Virginia's boys became President of the United States. **Washington, Jefferson, Madison, Monroe, William Henry Harrison, Tyler, Taylor,** and **Wilson** all were born in Virginia.

Close behind is Ohio, the birthplace of seven Presidents . . . **Grant, Hayes, Garfield, Benjamin Harrison, McKinley, Taft,** and **Harding.**

MOMMY, READ US THE STORY ABOUT THE OLD MAN WHO KNEW EVERYTHING

Louisa Adams, wife of **John Quincy Adams,** read the *Dialogues of Plato* to their sons in the original Greek.

THEY'RE YOUR RELATIVES

Mary Lincoln was suspected by many to have strong Southern sympathies. The suspicion was hardly without foundation. The reasons:

Her brother, George Todd, Surgeon, Confederate Army.

Her half brothers, David Todd, Samuel Todd, and Alexander Todd, all killed fighting in the Confederate Army.

Confederate Brigadier General Benjamin Hardin Helm, husband of her half sister Emilie, killed in action at the Battle of Chickamauga.

After her husband's death, Emilie went South from her home in Kentucky. Upon her return, she was refused readmission without first swearing an oath of allegiance to the United States. Emilie would not take the oath. The Union officer who was holding her in custody sent a telegram to Lincoln requesting instructions.

Lincoln wired back, "Send her to me."

So Emilie came to visit her sister and brother-in-law Abe at the White House, and the tongues wagged even faster than before.

STRANGE BEDFELLOWS

As part of Lady Bird Johnson's Beautification Program, the First Lady attended a ceremony dedicating the Astor Playground in New York. Later, en route to the reception, Mrs. Astor and Lady Bird shared a limousine. Chuckling, Mrs. Astor said, "Who would have ever thought I would be riding down Park Avenue with the First Lady of the Land!"

To which Mrs. Lyndon Johnson replied, "And who would have ever thought I would be riding down Park Avenue with Mrs. Astor!"

ONE MAN, ONE VOTE

Zachary Taylor never voted in a presidential election until he voted for himself.

ZACH'S SON-IN-LAW

The young lieutenant had served on **Zachary Taylor's** staff during the Mexican War. He was an outstanding soldier, but Zach didn't want him for a son-in-law. The general got him anyway when the lieutenant married Taylor's daughter Sarah, causing the usual family friction.

The young man was a central figure in a considerably bigger rift which occurred some years later. He was Jefferson Davis, President of the Confederate States of America.

THE PRESIDENTS

SISTERS UNDER THE SKIN?

Although Jackie Kennedy herself had been a reporter, she went to great lengths to avoid the press; but when she had to deal with them, she occasionally showed flashes of rather caustic humor.

Two female wire-service reporters, who were generally assigned to accompany her to church, were surprised to be accosted one Sunday by Secret Service agents, who said Mrs. Kennedy had told them "two strange Spanish-looking women" were after her.

When she returned to the White House on one occasion with a new German shepherd puppy, the press on Air Force One asked her what she would feed it.

"Reporters," she shot back.

At a crowded press reception in Paris, a *Women's Wear Daily* correspondent asked if she read that paper. Jackie replied, "I try not to."

REORIENTED

Helen Taft knew a good thing when she saw one. While her husband, **William Howard Taft,** was Governor General of the Philippines, the Tafts made a visit to Tokyo. Mrs. Taft was so impressed with the loveliness of the cherry trees there that later, as First Lady, she was instrumental in the gift of 3,000 Japanese cherry trees to Washington, where they were planted in 1912.

A long-time resident of Washington, Mrs. Taft, who died in 1943, enjoyed for many years the fruits of her efforts, the cherry blossoms blooming in the spring.

HOW TO ACHIEVE DETENTE

When the Russian Consul General rapes a 12-year-old girl, that's news, especially in Philadelphia in 1816. Ignorant of his diplomatic immunity, the local authorities, not surprisingly, put him in jail. President **James Madison** found out about it and told them they couldn't do that. The Consul General, Nicholas Kosloff, was released. By this time, however, his boss, Russian Minister André de Dashkoff, was so angry that his man had been jailed that he reported the breach of immunity to the Czar. Now the Czar got angry and banned the American chargé d'affaires in St. Petersburg from the Russian court.

When the Czar finally got the whole story, not just Dashkoff's version, he calmed down, restored the American chargé to official good graces and recalled his own men.

The Madisons could again serve caviar with a good conscience.

Tidbits & Trivia

SWEET WILLIAM

Life was harsh for many First Ladies . . . illnesses, loss of children, poverty, and the loneliness of women married to important men . . . but there were few among them who did not have solicitous husbands. Possibly the most solicitous of these was **William McKinley.**

Ida McKinley crocheted bedroom slippers, thousands and thousands of pairs of bedroom slippers, which she gave away. Ida McKinley was not well. Childless, depressed, epileptic, she was treated by her husband with great tenderness.

She insisted on being with him as much as possible and sat by his side at public functions, which she insisted on attending. Not infrequently, Ida McKinley would have a seizure, at which point the President would place a handkerchief over her face until it had passed. The discomfiture of those present may well be imagined.

"President McKinley," said his friend and political mentor, Mark Hanna, "has made it pretty hard for the rest of the husbands."

With the inner toughness of spirit that is sometimes surprising, Ida McKinley survived her husband's assassination for nearly six years.

WE OUGHT TO BE IN PICTURES

Patricia Ryan and Nancy Davis appeared in movies before they took husbands and started raising families. Pat Nixon was an extra in such films as *Ben Hur, The Great Ziegfeld* and *Becky Sharp*.

Nancy Reagan got her film start after appearing in a play called *Broken Dishes.* She went on to star in a number of films including *Donovan's Brain* and in her last picture *Hellcats of the Navy* (1956), she played opposite her husband. Both actresses gave up their glamorous careers and did not resume them until they went to Washington to become supporting players in the Capital's longest running melodrama.

THE FIRST

The first President married to a college graduate was **Rutherford B. Hayes.** His wife, Lucy, was graduated with highest honors from Ohio Wesleyan Women's College in 1850.

THAT'S WHAT'S UP, DOC

As the presidential election returns came in and it seemed certain that her husband, **John Kennedy,** would be the winner, Jacqueline Kennedy turned to him and said, "Oh, Bunny, you're President now."

TELL THAT TO YOUR HISTORY TEACHER

James K. Polk had a long-time intimate relationship with his secretary.

His secretary was a married woman.

Her name was Mrs. James K. Polk.

THE PRESIDENTS

"AND I SAY TO YOU . . ."

When it came to **Warren Harding's** speechmaking, William Gibbs McAdoo, Secretary of the Treasury under Woodrow Wilson, had a few things to say. Of Harding's speeches McAdoo commented:

"He spoke in a big bow-wow style of oratory. His speeches left the impression of an army of pompous phrases moving over the landscape in search of an idea; sometimes these meandering words would actually capture a straggling thought and bear it triumphantly, a prisoner in their midst, until it died of servitude and overwork."

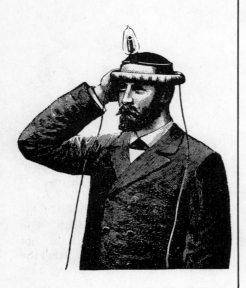

THE FIRST

The first President to visit the West Coast was **Rutherford B. Hayes,** who arrived in San Francisco, in September 1880.

HAIL TO THE CHEF

Thomas Jefferson set a magnificent table. At a time when a turkey cost 75¢ and a hog $3.00, he frequently spent as much as $50 a day on groceries. During his eight years in the White House, his wine bill alone was almost $11,000. The wines and many of the delicacies offered had been imported from Europe, and his chef came from France.

Jefferson was a food man. He wasn't a clothes man. Perhaps because he was a widower without a wife to enforce sartorial ground rules, he often entertained his guests wearing his old dressing gown and bedroom slippers.

The dining table was round, which discouraged formality. It was a rather first-come, first-served boardinghouse arrangement, which Jefferson called "pêle-mêle."

The person most upset by this congenial approach was protocol-minded British Ambassador Anthony Merry. Following one of Jefferson's dinner parties, Merry reported angrily of having headed for an empty place and losing the seat to a member of the House of Representatives who was faster.

PRESIDENTS ON THE PRESIDENCY

I think the American public wants a solemn ass as President and I think I'll go along with them.

Calvin Coolidge

ON THE MENU

The Republicans were so delighted to be back in office in 1889 that the menu at **Benjamin Harrison's** inaugural ball made it clear who was in charge. Served were such treats as Pâté de foie gras á la Harrison, Terrine of game á la Morton (the Vice President) and a "beehive of bon-bons Republican."

PRESIDENTS ON THE PRESIDENCY

I enjoy being President, and I like to do the work and have my hand on the lever.

Theodore Roosevelt

Tidbits & Trivia

NAME ME A PRESIDENT AND I'LL NAME YOU A GOOD SPORT

Everyone knows that **Teddy Roosevelt** liked to hunt, that **F. D. Roosevelt** liked to sail, and **D. Eisenhower** preferred golf, but what about some of the other popular sports for Presidents? Who was into croquet? **Ruther-**

SUPERFLUOUS

A friend tried to persuade **Ulysses S. Grant** to take up golf as a good form of exercise. Grant consented to be an observer.

Arriving at the course, the first thing they saw was a tyro swinging his driver vigorously but vainly.

"That does look like very good exercise," agreed Grant. "What is the little white ball for?"

LASSOED!

When **William McKinley** died and **Teddy Roosevelt** became President, Senator Mark Hanna, close friend and confidant of McKinley exclaimed, "Now that damn cowboy is in the White House."

HEADY REMARK

Lyndon Johnson on Jerry Ford: "Jerry is a nice guy but he played too much football with his helmet off."

ford B. Hayes, that's who. Who liked to toss Indian clubs? **Cal Coolidge** is the one. Cal also rode the mechanical horse, but for a fine warm day spent in the country he liked nothing better than pitching hay. **Hoover** got the kinks out by using a medicine ball.

Kennedy, despite a bad back, liked touch football and **Carter** took up both tennis and jogging. **Reagan** does his riding on a real horse.

BETTER THAN PAR FOR THE COURSE

On February 6, 1968, while playing golf at Palm Springs, California, **Dwight D. Eisenhower** scored a hole-in-one.

THREE STRIKES, YOU'RE OUT!

Harry Truman loved the opening day of baseball season. It gave him a chance to show off. (He was ambidextrous and could throw out the ball with either hand.) Kennedy liked it too; he brought his entire family and showed *them* off. Nixon, however, could not have cared less. He liked the game, but preferred watching it on TV.

THE PRESIDENTS

When serving as a general **Zachary Taylor** usually wore a wide-brimmed straw hat, baggy pants stuffed into his boots, and a plain coat without insignia of rank. If he was going to be in battle, at least he was going to be comfortable.

A thoroughly unmilitary figure, except for his results, Taylor was so heavy and his legs so short that he had to be boosted onto his horse.

After he was elected President, Taylor didn't change his manner of dress. Only his costume. He wore black suits that were deliberately cut too large so that they would be plenty roomy and high silk hats which he wore tilted on the back of his head.

PRESIDENTS ON THE PRESIDENCY
"No man who ever held the office of President would congratulate a friend on obtaining it."
John Adams

ENTER HELEN AND DICK

Helen Taft made swift changes in the White House staff, to the embarrassment of Edith Roosevelt, whose housekeeping habits she criticized, and to the misfortune of the old retainers, whom she fired.

"Mrs. Taft," said Mary Randolph, secretary to six First Ladies, "replaced the ancient ushers who wore frocked coats and looked like characters out of a Dickens story."

Helen's idea of proper servants were liveried doormen and a formally uniformed staff.

Years later, **Richard Nixon** was criticized for a similar move, when he tried to dress the White House guard with European pomp, plumes and pageantry.

TELLING TAILS

When pianist Van Cliburn arrived in Washington for a concert minus his suitcase, he called a friend to try to borrow a set of tails and wound up with President **Lyndon B. Johnson's**. It took a major pin-up job, because the President was a good deal heavier, but at least the length was right!

SUIT THYSELF

Among the more nattily dressed Presidents were **Martin Van Buren** and **Chester A. Arthur.**

If it is true that clothes make the man, occasionally the opposite is true. Originally a tailor by trade, President **Andrew Johnson** had all his clothes custom-made by President Andrew Johnson.

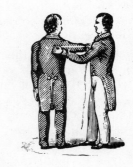

PRESIDENT WHO?

"When they say 'Mister President'" **William Howard Taft** admitted not long after his election, "I always look around and expect to see Roosevelt!"

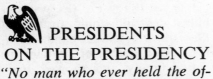

Tidbits & Trivia

MOMENT OF TRUTH

Harry Truman was summoned urgently to the White House and told the devastating news of **Franklin Roosevelt's** death by Mrs. Roosevelt. Truman later described himself as feeling at that moment "as though the moon and all the planets and all the stars had fallen upon me." At first he could not speak. When he could, he asked, "Is there anything I can do for you?"

"Is there anything *we* can do for *you?*" she said. "For you are the one in trouble now."

DEMOCRAT WITH A REPUBLICAN MEMORY

Many years after **Franklin Roosevelt's** decision to remain married to Eleanor although she offered to divorce him so that he could marry Lucy Mercer, Eleanor's secretary, Eleanor said to friends about the relationship:

"I have the memory of an elephant. I can forgive, but I cannot forget."

AND DON'T FORGET THE TRAVELERS CHECKS

The President who traveled outside the country most frequently while in office was the one who was physically the most immobile. **Franklin D. Roosevelt** made 24 trips out of the United States during his presidency.

FOUR GENTLEMEN FROM ALBANY

Martin Van Buren, Grover Cleveland, Theodore Roosevelt, and **Franklin Roosevelt** all served as Governor of New York before becoming President.

THAT OLD MASS MEDIUM

On the day of Franklin Roosevelt's death, there was scarcely a radio in the land that wasn't tuned in to the saddening news and every scrap and fragment of information connected with it.

But in New York City, on the lower East Side, one radio was silent. It was on a shelf in a small store, and when a customer entered he asked the old woman behind the counter why she didn't have the radio on.

"For what do I need the radio," replied the old woman. "It's on everybody's face."

THE PRESIDENTS

THE LONG, THE SHORT AND THE TALL

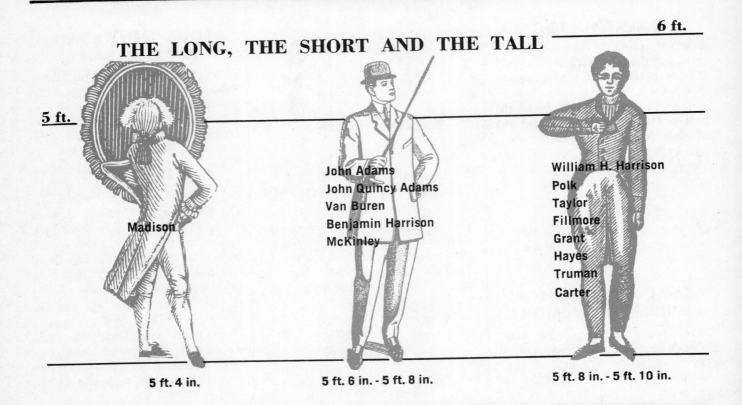

6 ft.

5 ft.

Madison

John Adams
John Quincy Adams
Van Buren
Benjamin Harrison
McKinley

William H. Harrison
Polk
Taylor
Fillmore
Grant
Hayes
Truman
Carter

5 ft. 4 in.   5 ft. 6 in. - 5 ft. 8 in.   5 ft. 8 in. - 5 ft. 10 in.

WELL-QUALIFIED

In 1888, an official campaign biography was written for **Benjamin Harrison** by a Hoosier neighbor. The neighbor was General Lou Wallace, already famous as the author of the celebrated novel "Ben Hur." One of Harrison's friends felt that the selection of Wallace as a biographer was a particularly good choice. As the gentleman put it, "He did so well on 'Ben Hur' that we surely can trust Wallace with 'Ben Him'."

PAY CLOSE ATTENTION

James Monroe's seventh annual message to Congress, delivered on December 2, 1823, included reports on finances, military affairs, and generally routine matters. Among the other information he presented, the President made two references to American foreign policy, one early in the speech, the other near the close.

Adroitly avoiding foreign repercussion by the apparent casualness of the references, the President had issued one of the strongest statements of intent which has ever been made in the history of American government. The two parts of the speech, put together, are the Monroe Doctrine.

CONVERSATIONAL CONSERVATIONIST

"I do not choose to run for President in 1928," said **Calvin Coolidge,** a statement that has been remembered ever since for both its brevity and its wisdom.

Coolidge wasted nothing, words included.

"I bet someone that I could get more than two words out of you," a visitor once said to him. Silent Cal did not speak. Then he did speak.

"You lose."

98

Tidbits & Trivia

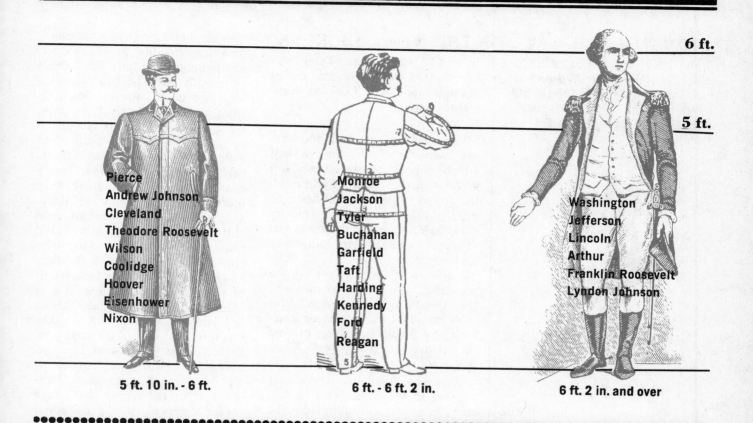

Pierce
Andrew Johnson
Cleveland
Theodore Roosevelt
Wilson
Coolidge
Hoover
Eisenhower
Nixon

Monroe
Jackson
Tyler
Buchanan
Garfield
Taft
Harding
Kennedy
Ford
Reagan

Washington
Jefferson
Lincoln
Arthur
Franklin Roosevelt
Lyndon Johnson

6 ft.

5 ft.

5 ft. 10 in. - 6 ft.

6 ft. - 6 ft. 2 in.

6 ft. 2 in. and over

HE KNEW HIS FATHER WELL

Young Calvin Coolidge, Jr., must have been a chip off the old block when it came to plain talk. President **Coolidge** recalled that on the day he became President, his young son had just started to work in a tobacco field. "When one of the laborers said to him, 'If my father was President I would not work in a tobacco field,' Young Cal replied, 'If my father were your father, you would!'"

PIPE DOWN!!!

The inadequacies of the White House plumbing were good-naturedly discussed by several Presidents in the early days of indoor "conveniences," but **Theodore Roosevelt's** clan knew the *real* truth about the temperamental pipes.

When the water ran out of the great tub, T.R., Jr., recalled that the drainpipe made "the most astonishing series of gurgles." But, he went on, "We were told by our Irish nurse not to worry, that these were outcries of the 'faucet lady' and we watched with care to see if we could catch a glimpse of her head in the pipe!"

WHAT'S YOUR NAME, LITTLE BOY?

A White House visitor asked **Dwight Eisenhower's** young grandson, David, what his name was.

"Dwight David Eisenhower," the boy replied.

The President was seated nearby. "If you are Dwight David Eisenhower," said the visitor, gesturing toward the President, "then who is he?"

David answered without hesitation. "That's Ike," he said.

99

THE PRESIDENTS

INDIAN LOVE CALL

Only sixteen months after his first wife died, **Woodrow Wilson** married an attractive widow, Mrs. Edith Bolling Galt, a ninth-generation direct descendant of Princess Pocahontas.

FLO'S FOLLIES

Mrs. Harding had the White House silver triple gold-plated.

THE VERY DICKENS

In 1841, when **John Tyler** was President, Charles Dickens called at the White House. Dickens' comments appear in his *American Notes*.

"We entered a large hall, and having twice or thrice rung a bell which nobody answered, walked without further ceremony through the rooms on the ground floor, as diverse other gentlemen (mostly with their hats on, and their hands in their pockets) were doing very leisurely . . .

"A few were closely eyeing the movables, as if to make quite sure that the President (who was far from popular) had not made away with any of the furniture, or sold the fixtures for his private benefit . . .

"There were some fifteen or twenty persons in the room. One, a tall, wiry, muscular old man, from the west; sunburned and swarthy . . . who sat bolt upright in his chair, frowning steadily at the carpet, and twitching the hard lines about his mouth, as if he had made up his mind to 'fix' the President on what he had to say. . . . Another, a Kentucky farmer, six-feet-six in height . . . who leaned against the wall and kicked the floor with his heels, as though he had Time's head under his shoe, and were literally "killing" him. A third, an oval-faced bilious-looking man with . . . whiskers and beard shaved down to blue dots, who sucked the head of a thick stick, and from time to time took it out of his mouth, to see how it was getting on. A fourth did nothing but whistle. A fifth did nothing but spit. And indeed all these gentlemen were so persevering and energetic in this latter particular, and bestowed their favors so abundantly upon the carpet, that I take it for granted the presidential housemaids have high wages."

Tidbits & Trivia

HOUSE WAS NOT A HOME

After a private tour of the White House conducted by outgoing First Lady Mamie Eisenhower for incoming First Lady Jacqueline Kennedy, Jackie cried hysterically, telling an aide the place looked like a hotel that had been decorated by a wholesale furniture store during a January clearance.

STOVE IN

Until **Millard Fillmore** became President in 1850, all White House cooking had been done over open fireplaces. Clearly a man who did not like all his food charcoal broiled, Fillmore purchased a cast-iron stove.

Since no list of instructions was provided, even though the stove worked, the cook wouldn't.

Fillmore solved the crisis of the kitchen by going to the U.S. Patent Office, studying a model of the stove, and personally instructing the cook in the mysteries of its operation.

ALOHA!

When Queen Emma of the Sandwich Islands, now known as Hawaii, arrived to pay her respects to **Andrew Johnson** in 1866, he became the first President to receive the visit of a Queen.

HEATING UP A WARM RECEPTION

A variety of assorted guests were invited to the White House during the administration of **James Buchanan.**

One was Bertie, Prince of Wales, the future Edward VII, who slept in Buchanan's room while Buchanan spent the night on a sofa.

On another occasion there was a large delegation from Japan, the first such group ever sent abroad by that nation.

And then there was the young Indian brave who was somewhat less than impressed by his illustrious surroundings. In fact, he took the occasion to deliver a few words at a high decibel level to the effect that the White House belonged to the Indians, the ground it stood on belonged to the Indians, and that personally he was prepared to fight to get them back.

The President, a man whose record shows that a fight was something that he wanted no part of, calmed his guest with a few platitudes about brotherhood. The young brave remained at the reception, there was no fight, and the White House still belongs to the Indians only in the sense that it belongs to all the American people.

THE PRESIDENTS

JOANIE WHO?

Insiders said that **Jimmy Carter** looked over running mates' wives as carefully as the would-be candidates themselves. Joan and Walter Mondale, both preachers' kids, were naturals. "Mondale's wife has never interfered and is known for two things," said the Congressional Doorkeeper: "eternal optimism and a good, clean, shiny house."

HE BLOVIATED IN PUBLIC

Warren Harding had the ability to bloviate whenever he wanted to. He was a master at bloviating. He should have been, for he'd created the term himself. Bloviating is the art of speaking, for as long as the occasion warrants, and saying nothing . . . praising all the good things, damning all the bad things, and revealing one's own position on not a single one.

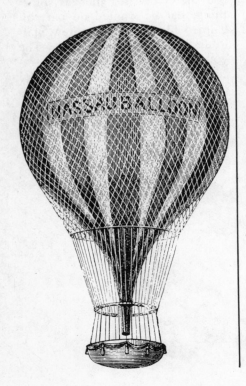

"I REGRET THAT I HAVE BUT ONE LIFE . . ."

When the Secret Service, on an **LBJ** trip to Samoa, refused to let the President drink ceremonial kava-kava with the island's chiefs, a major diplomatic crisis loomed.

An official "taster," someone expendable, was sought for the job, and Lady Bird Johnson stepped forward, sipping kava-kava like a veteran with Samoan chieftains.

It was reported that she slept most of the way to New Zealand, the next stop on the President's itinerary.

TELL IT TO THE IRS

During **Grover Cleveland's** Second Term, on May 20, 1895, the Income Tax was declared unconstitutional.

THE FIRST

The first President to broadcast from the White House over television was **Harry Truman,** in 1947.

WE'LL MAKE YOU A STAR!!!

President **Eisenhower** was the first President to use makeup for his TV appearances, a judicious application of pancake supervised by noneother than his actor friend, Robert Montgomery.

Kennedy preferred daily use of a sunlamp to give him that healthy glow under the camera's lights, but **LBJ** used makeup, especially under the eyes.

It was **Nixon's** pallor and heavy beard that didn't do much for his TV image, with or without pancake.

Jerry Ford reluctantly agreed to use "just a little."

Tidbits & Trivia

HOW WELL HE KNEW

Inaugurated as Vice-President under Woodrow Wilson, Thomas Marshall displayed a complete grasp of the position he was about to assume:

"I believe I'm entitled to make a few remarks," the new Vice-President said as he began his address, "because I'm about to enter a four-year period of silence."

GOLDEN GIRL

Teddy Roosevelt had set up a separate trust fund for Alice, the daughter of his first wife. When he suffered financial reverses in the winter of 1887, he told Edith, his second wife, only half jokingly, "Be nice to Alice. We might have to borrow money from her one day."

I'M NEVER WRONG

In 1920, Henry Cabot Lodge, Sr., the powerful and patrician Republican Senator from Massachusetts, offered his opinion of **Franklin D. Roosevelt,** at that time Democratic candidate for Vice-President. Said Lodge of Roosevelt,

"He is a well-meaning, nice young fellow, but light."

LET THEM WEAR PANTS

As far back as 1915, Alice Roosevelt Longworth wore slacks in public and predicted a rosy future for the new style.

"I urge all the ladies to wear pantalettes," she said. "They're comfortable, economical and save considerable cloth."

THEY REMEMBER FRANK, HANK AND NAT IN BRUNSWICK

Franklin Pierce was a graduate of Bowdoin College, Brunswick, Maine, Class of 1824. Among his schoolmates and friends at Bowdoin were Henry Wadsworth Longfellow and Nathaniel Hawthorne.

Still friends 40 years later, Pierce and Hawthorne went off on a vacation to the White Mountains. Hawthorne, author of such illustrious works as *The Scarlet Letter* and *The House of Seven Gables,* wrote a sad ending to the vacation by (as he might have put it himself) succumbing.

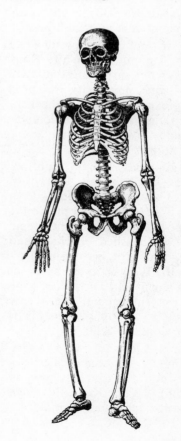

THE PRESIDENTS

PREXY'S PETS

From time to time Americans have held the belief that there was a jackass in the White House. That's entirely possible.

George Washington treated his horses as if they were members of the First Family; **Teddy Roosevelt's** kids played with a one-legged rooster and took their pony up and down in the White House elevator; **Woodrow Wilson** admired the sheep on the White House lawn; **William Howard Taft** had a cow named Pauline; and **Warren Harding** enjoyed training dogs to sit on chairs and perform at cabinet meetings.

Dogs, in fact, win paws-down as the most popular of White House pets. It's not surprising that **Richard Nixon's** popularity was probably greatest after his "Checkers" speech, during which he defended a child's love of a dog, among other things.

John Kennedy, though reportedly allergic to dog's hair, was visibly fond of man's best friend — to the point that, one day stepping out of the pool and into some doggie litter, he flashed a charismatic smile, and kept his comments to himself. It was even said that when Khrushchev and Cuban missiles were menacing, JFK seemed to gain solace in petting his favorite dog, "Charlie."

When "the Russians were coming" (Pushinka, daughter of the Soviet space dog Khrushchev, was expecting), Jackie Kennedy herself cut strips of paper to make soft beds for the newborn pups.

LBJ, the big Texan who did things in a big way, did them even bigger when it came to his beloved hounds. When "Old Beagle" died, the President had the pooch cremated. The ashes were temporarily stored in a box on top of the refrigerator.

Bianca, another LBJ dog, was openly jealous of the attention the master lavished on "Him," his favorite beagle. The haughty canine was so vexed that after an arts festival she watered a piece of sculpture by Alexander Calder that was on loan to the White House from the Museum of Modern Art in New York.

Edgar, on the other hand, was something else. An FBI "agent" with a damp nose, the dog was a gift from J. Edgar Hoover to LBJ. LBJ's prima donna dog, Bianca, apparently didn't think much of "the spy who came in from the cold," and bit Edgar so soundly he needed stitches.

Another LBJ canine, Yuki, had plastic boots that it wore in the rain. LBJ once shook Yuki's hand at a reception for top military brass. Then he shook the hands of the officers.

Patricia Nixon had less luck when she was introduced to the new presidential pooch, King Timahoe. The big Irish setter knocked her down three times.

All Presidents, whether or not they really loved dogs, fully understood their public appeal: JFK was delighted at Pushinka's intelligence and had the dog handler teach her how to climb the ladder to Caroline's tree house. When the pooch finally made it, Kennedy's intuitive political shutter clicked along with the cameras while he grinned, "That's worth six million votes right there!"

"Dog" days cost votes, too, such as LBJ's controversial handling of his dogs when he picked them up by their ears. Worse yet, when the District of Columbia Dog Tag #1 was issued to the beagle "Him" and Dog Tag #2 to "Her," the press called to ask in all seriousness, "How do you reconcile this with the President's pledge to give women equal opportunity?"

Tidbits & Trivia

GENERAL INFORMATION

Among the Presidents there were twelve men who had served as generals:

Commander-in-Chief:
    Washington
General of the Armies:
    Eisenhower
General: **Grant**
Major General: **Jackson**
                   W. Harrison
                   Taylor
                   Garfield
Brigadier General: **Pierce**
Brigadier General, U.S.
    Volunteers: **Andrew Johnson**
Brevet Major General: **Hayes**
Brevet Brigadier General:
    Benjamin Harrison
Quartermaster General (rank of
    Brigadier General): **Arthur**

There have been no former admirals among the Presidents.

TACT

Robert E. Lee used to tell an army story about **Zachary Taylor.** Taylor was serving as a general in the Mexican War when a young officer galloped up to the General's headquarters and announced that he had just seen 20,000 Mexicans with 250 guns marching in the direction of the American forces.

"You saw 20,000 men?" inquired Taylor.

"Yes."

"With 250 guns?"

"Yes, yes."

"Well, then I must believe you," said the General, "but I would not have believed it if I had seen it myself."

MEDICALLY UNCERTAIN

On July 4, 1850, President **Zachary Taylor** attended a cornerstone-laying ceremony at the unfinished Washington Monument. The day was very hot.

When the ceremony was over, Taylor returned to the White House, drank cold milk, ate cherries, got sick, and died on July 9.

The exact cause of his death never has been determined. It was, one may speculate, attributable to the milk, the cherries, or the ceremony.

THE PRESIDENTS

OBITUARIES

*A compendium of unfortunate demises
which occurred
during presidential terms of office*

PRESIDENTS

Assassinations

	Date of Occurrence	Died	Age	Served as President
Abraham Lincoln	April 14, 1865	April 15, 1865	56	4 years, 42 days
James Garfield	July 2, 1881	September 19, 1881	49	199 days
William McKinley	September 6, 1901	September 14, 1901	58	4 years, 194 days
John F. Kennedy	November 22, 1963	November 22, 1963	46	2 years, 306 days

Natural Causes

		Died	Age	Served as President
William Henry Harrison		April 4, 1841	68	32 days
Zachary Taylor		July 9, 1850	65	1 year, 127 days
Warren Harding		August 2, 1923	57	2 years, 151 days
Franklin D. Roosevelt		April 12, 1945	63	12 years, 39 days

FIRST LADIES

	Husband's Term	Died	Age
Letitia Tyler (Mrs. John)	April 6, 1841 - March 3, 1845	September 10, 1842	51
Caroline Harrison (Mrs. Benjamin)	March 4, 1889 - March 3, 1893	October 25, 1892	60
Ellen Wilson (Mrs. Woodrow)	March 4, 1913 - March 3, 1921	August 6, 1914	54

CHILDREN

	Parents	Father's Term	Died	Age
Charles Adams	John and Abigail	March 4, 1797 - March 3, 1801	November 30, 1800	20
Mary Jefferson	Thomas and Martha (deceased)	March 4, 1801 - March 3, 1809	April 17, 1804	25
William Wallace Lincoln	Abraham and Mary	March 4, 1861 - April 15, 1865	February 20, 1862	11
Calvin Coolidge, Jr.	Calvin, Sr. and Grace	August 3, 1923 - March 3, 1929	July 7, 1924	16
Patrick Bouvier Kennedy	John and Jacqueline	January 20, 1961 - November 22, 1963	August 9, 1963	2 days

Tidbits & Trivia

TO RACHEL, TO ELLEN

Presidents **Andrew Jackson,** "Old Hickory," and "Gentleman Boss" **Chester A. Arthur,** a sophisticated, dapper, handsome veteran of New York machine politics, had one thing in common: love. Both entered the presidential office as widowers, both had adored their wives, and both followed a daily ritual of remembrance during their White House years.

Jackson wore an ivory miniature of his late wife, Rachel, around his neck, removing it at night and placing it beside his bed so that it was the first thing he saw when he awoke in the morning.

Arthur placed a bouquet of fresh flowers next to his Ellen's photograph each day.

Although they did not live to share their husbands' attainment of the highest office in the land, somehow, somewhere, Rachel Jackson and Ellen Arthur must have known what every woman knows.

ANYTHING MISSING HERE?

Thomas Jefferson wrote his own epitaph. It reads:

"Here was buried Thomas Jefferson, author of the Declaration of Independence, of the Statute of Virginia for Religious Freedom, and the father of the University of Virginia."

Tom either forgot, which was not like Tom, or chose to exclude the fact that he'd also been President of the United States.

EVEN ON SUNDAY

The people really got their money's worth out of President **James Polk**. He worked hard every day during his four years as President and never took time off. He didn't go fishing. He didn't play golf. He didn't even steal away for long weekends. What's more, his wife worked right along with him, side by side, helping run the country.

He left office with a great sigh of relief, and died three months later.

UNHAPPY PRESENCE

Robert Lincoln, the President's eldest son, was called to his father's side on the night of Lincoln's assassination, April 14, 1865.

Fifteen years later, on July 2, 1881, while serving as Secretary of War in the Garfield administration, he was to accompany Garfield on a trip. He arrived at the Washington railroad station as Garfield was being assassinated there.

Twenty years later, Robert Lincoln was invited to the Pan-American Exposition in Buffalo. On September 6, 1901, he was not far from the Exposition grounds when the third presidential assassination, that of William McKinley, took place.

THE PRESIDENTS

STONEWALL NIXON

Relations were never cordial between **Richard Nixon** and the press, but from time to time his press secretary, Ron Zeigler, would hint that a great quote was forthcoming.

In China with the presidential party, Zeigler told reporters, "If you ask the President how he likes the Great Wall, he will be prepared to answer."

Dutifully, the correspondents inquired, "How do you like the Great Wall, Mr. President?"

Nixon looked obligingly up at the ancient wonder of the world and said, "I must say that the Great Wall is a great wall."

NO WONDER HE DIDN'T HAVE MUCH RESPECT FOR HARVARD TYPES

He worked hard in high school and really hit the books. His penchant for long hours of study would later win him the nickname "Iron Pants." At the end of his high school years, the drive to succeed won him top honors of his class. He was awarded the Harvard Club of California prize as the most outstanding all-around student. What was the prize? A biography of a little-known Harvard dean. Hardly a reward worthy of the effort put out by **Richard Milhous Nixon**, class of 1930, Whittier High.

RESIGNED TO IT

Richard M. Nixon may have been the first President to resign, but a century and a half before, the first Vice-President resigned. He was John Caldwell Calhoun, who had served as **John Quincy Adams'** number-two man from March 4, 1825, to March 4, 1829, and **Andrew Jackson's** Veep from March 4, 1829, to December 28, 1832, when he resigned. The reason? He had been elected Senator from South Carolina. Obviously, a position with a lot more prestige than the vice-presidency.

PAT ON THE PRESS

Mrs. Nixon did not have the same difficulties with the media that her husband had. She told her assistant to "treat them with kid gloves and butter them up."

ASK MOM

About her son, Hannah Nixon commented:

"People seldom dictate to Richard."

FAMOUS LAST WORDS

Nixon to Haldeman, April 25, 1973:

"You know, I always wondered about that taping equipment, but I'm damn glad we have it, aren't you?"

Tidbits & Trivia

THERE WAS A LOT OF FIRING THAT YEAR

Herbert Hoover was an extremely successful mining engineer, and his profession took him to many places around the world. In 1900, while working for the Chinese Bureau of Mines in Tientsen, he was caught in the Boxer Rebellion. For weeks the city was under siege. Finally Hoover felt that it had been strongly suggested "by way of artillery" that his services were no longer required.

LOST IN THE ZEROES

$$0\,0\,0,0\,0\,0,0\,0\,0$$

Some time after he left office and the national debt had more than doubled, **Herbert Hoover** commented on that poor creature, the decimal point, "wandering around among the regimented ciphers trying to find some of the old places it used to know."

MR. EX-PRESIDENT

James K. Polk scarcely had time to enjoy his retirement from the presidency. Worn out from overwork during his single term in office, he lived for only three months, an ex-President for the shortest time.

Herbert Hoover, who left office under a cloud of criticism in the Great Depression, lived long enough to become revered as an elder statesman and political sage by the time he died. He had been an ex-President for the longest time, 31 years.

FORTUNATELY, THINGS GOT BETTER

Father died when he was six. Mother died when he was eight. **Herbert Hoover** was an orphan.

ON HER HONOR

Lou Hoover was a good scout. A very good scout. She was such a good scout that she served as President of the Girl Scouts of America.

THE PRESIDENTS

PRESIDENTIAL STAKES RACE:
RENOMINATED BUT NOT REELECTED

Past performance does not always help in figuring the odds on returning an incumbent or former President to the White House. Here are the entries and results of ten runnings of the Washingtonian National. In each race a challenger finished in front of a President.

P Incumbent or former President

Race	Entries	Results
1800	**P** J. Adams T. Jefferson A. Burr	Jefferson outran Adams easily, but stablemate Burr's unexpected run for the wire threw race into dead heat. Race stewards in H. of Rep. gave call to "Long Tom."
1840	**P** M. Van Buren W. Harrison J. Birney	Spirited ride by "Old Tip" wins it in a no-issue race. Van Buren used up in mud. Birney showed nothing.
1856	**P** M. Fillmore[1] J. Buchanan J. Frémont **P** F. Pierce[2]	Fillmore left at the gate. Frémont ran well in new Republican silks but could not hold off the favorite, Buchanan, in stretch drive.
1888	**P** G. Cleveland B. Harrison C. Fisk A. Streeter	Cleveland thrown off stride by interference. Harrison takes it in close one. Fisk no threat. Streeter out of it.
1892	**P** B. Harrison J. Weaver G. Cleveland J. Bidwell	Harrison's turn to trail a stronger Cleveland. Weaver's third-party effort impressive. Bidwell (Prohibition) ran dry.
1912	**P** W. Taft **P** T. Roosevelt W. Wilson E. Debs E. Chafin	Roosevelt, a late entry, bulled his way on inside after trying to bump Taft. Wilson moved to lead and won easily. Debs game in third-time try. Chafin no factor.
1932	**P** H. Hoover F. Roosevelt N. Thomas	Roosevelt took lead early and won easily with Hoover way back. Thomas ran too wide to be a factor.
1976	**P** G. Ford J. Carter R. Reagan[3] McCarthy	Carter, running from good post position after string of claiming races, moved to an early lead. Ford, tired from fighting off Reagan in the GOP trial, was not able to head Carter in the stretch drive. McCarthy out of it.
1980	**P** J. Carter R. Reagan J. Anderson	Lackluster three-way race that tipsters could not call. Carter slow to leave garden gate. Spoiler bid by Anderson fails. Reagan takes it easily despite age.

[1]Lost Whig renomination in 1852, now running under Know-Nothing colors

[2]Incumbent scratched by Dems as not strong enough to win

[3]Reagan received 1 Electoral Vote

Tidbits & Trivia

A HARD LETTER TO WRITE

Abraham Lincoln's touching humanity was as well known as his ability to move people by the simple direct way in which he expressed himself. This letter of condolence to Mrs. Bixby is a case in point.

Executive Mansion
Washington, Nov. 21, 1864

Dear Madam, —

I have been shown in the files of the War Department a statement of the Adjutant General of Massachusetts, that you are the mother of five sons who have died gloriously on the field of battle.

I feel how weak and fruitless must be any word of mine which should attempt to beguile you from the grief of a loss so overwhelming. But I cannot refrain from tendering to you the consolation that may be found in the thanks of the Republic they died to save.

I pray that our Heavenly Father may assuage the anguish of your bereavement, and leave you only the cherished memory of the loved and lost, and the solemn pride that must be yours, to have laid so costly a sacrifice upon the altar of Freedom.

Yours, very sincerely and respectfully,

A. Lincoln

Five months later Lincoln was assassinated. There was no second Lincoln to help relieve the nation's anguish.

A STEADY HAND

On January 1, 1863, **Abraham Lincoln** signed the Emancipation Proclamation freeing the slaves. His signature was firm and bold, but writing it had been no easy matter.

The President had attended a White House New Year's reception earlier that day and shaken hands with hundreds of visitors. As a result, his own hand was still stiff and sore when he took the pen to sign the document.

Totally committed to the concept of emancipation and certain of his resolve, Lincoln knew that his signature on a document that would change the course of history must not look hesitant and unsure. If it did, he himself would appear uncertain and unsure of the step he was taking. Slowly, painfully, and with great care, he signed his name.

THE PRESIDENTS

THE SIMPLE TRUTH

Martha Patterson served her father as First Lady, since her mother was an invalid.

When the family entered the White House, Martha said, "We are plain people from the mountains of Tennessee. I trust too much will not be expected of us."

Apparently no one was listening. Expectations so exceeded the performance of her father, **Andrew Johnson,** that he became the only President ever to be impeached.

UNIMPEACHABLE CHARACTER

Six years after he left Washington under a cloud, ex-President **Andrew Johnson** returned in triumph. The newly-elected Senator from Tennessee, the only ex-President to be elected to the Senate, Johnson entered the Senate Chamber to find his desk covered with flowers. He was greeted warmly by many of his new associates and an enthusiastic gallery.

Senator Oliver P. Morton, however, turned his face away in embarrassment. Once a friend and supporter of Johnson, he had played turncoat during Johnson's impeachment trial and voted for conviction.

Johnson looked for Morton and found him. The Senator from Tennessee extended his hand. The Senator from Indiana took it gladly.

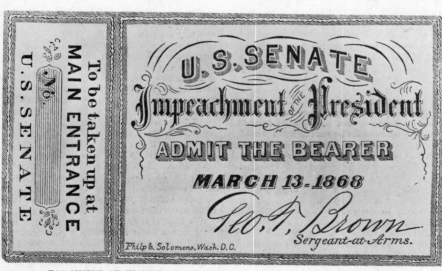

U.S. SENATE
To be taken up at MAIN ENTRANCE
CA. No.
U.S. SENATE

U.S. SENATE
Impeachment of the President
ADMIT THE BEARER
MARCH 13. 1868
Geo. T. Brown
Sergeant-at-Arms.
Philp & Solomons, Wash. D.C.

FAC-SIMILE OF TICKET OF ADMISSION TO THE IMPEACHMENT TRIAL.

AND THEN HE KNEW

It was 11:02 A.M. when Vice-President **Gerald Ford** walked into President **Nixon's** Oval Office. "You will do a good job, Jerry," said Nixon.

That's how Ford found out Nixon was going to resign the presidency that evening, August 9, 1974.

INDIRECT APPROACH

How many popular votes does a man need to be President? It can be done with as few as none. **Gerald Ford** did it.

While Ford has been the only President to be appointed, actually we all did vote for him indirectly. We elected the Congressmen who, in turn, chose Ford. We elected. They selected.

I BEG YOUR PARDON

Gerald Ford's pardon of his predecessor, Richard Nixon, probably cost Ford election as President in his own right, but he always believed he had done the right thing.

As for Nixon, he called the pardon "the most humiliating day of my life."

Tidbits & Trivia

BUT WHO'S COUNTING

It's much more common than most people realize for a man to be elected President without receiving a majority of the popular vote. This has happened fifteen times, generally when a number of candidates were running.

Presidents elected without receiving a popular majority:

John Quincy Adams, James K. Polk, Zachary Taylor, James Buchanan, Abraham Lincoln (first term), **Rutherford B. Hayes, James A. Garfield, Grover Cleveland** (both terms), **Benjamin Harrison, Woodrow Wilson** (both terms), **Harry S. Truman, John F. Kennedy, Richard M. Nixon** (first term), and **James E. Carter.**

THE WHIGS ARE GONE, BUT THE PHRASE ROLLS ON

Among the banners, buttons, and other assorted electioneering paraphernalia of **William Henry Harrison's** cider and log cabin campaign of 1840 one item stood out, quite literally. It was a ball, a paper ball, perhaps six feet in diameter, inscribed with Whig political slogans. During the campaign, Harrison's followers pushed the huge ball from city to city, shouting what in effect became an additional slogan, "Keep the ball rolling!"

Long gone, the Whigs have left us the phrase as their legacy.

BIG YEAR FOR PRESIDENTS

On two separate occasions the country had three Presidents in one year.

In 1841, on March 3, **Martin Van Buren** completed his term of office. **William Henry Harrison** was inaugurated, died a month later, and **John Tyler** became President.

It happened again in 1881. **Rutherford B. Hayes'** term ended on March 3 and **James Garfield** became President. Garfield was shot in July, died in September, and **Chester A. Arthur** became the third President of that year.

113

THE PRESIDENTS

MAGNIFICENT DOLL

Washington Irving, the colorful chronicler of Washington's early days, described **Dolley** and **James Madison** in terms that fit them perfectly. Dolley, he wrote, is a "fine, portly, buxom dame." And her husband, James? "Jemmy, ah, poor Jemmy," lamented Irving. "He is but a withered little apple-john."

DON'T FORGET THE "E"

Dolley Madison's real name was Dolley — with an "E." Nobody told the ice cream people.

TIMES HAVEN'T CHANGED MUCH

When Dolley Madison was First Lady, she bought an imported mirror for $40 to hang in the White House.

The Senate, infuriated that she had purchased the item from abroad, launched an investigation into the matter. The investigation cost $2,000.

AND JOHNNY CAME MARCHING HOME

John Adams did everything he could to recall his Minister to Prussia. He sent five letters of recall overseas in January 1801, hoping at least one would be received promptly. One letter finally reached the Minister in April. It read, "It is my opinion this minister ought to be recalled from Prussia . . . it is my duty to call him home."

In September, nine months after the recall was issued, the Minister finally returned to the United States. He was **John Quincy Adams**, the President's son.

HERE A CANE, THERE A CANE, EVERYWHERE A CANE, CANE

Presidents may or may not have had large estates to pass on to their heirs, but what they have had, in great abundance, are an assortment of canes, walking sticks, staffs and the like to bequeath, bequest and bestow on relatives, friends and admirers.

For canes, with the possible exception of slaves (!) appear to have been bequeathed by Presidents more than any other object, in spite of the fact they went out of fashion with **Benjamin Harrison**.

Some canes have even been left twice, like the one **George Washington** left his brother Charles — it had been left to George by Ben Franklin in 1790. And **Thomas Jefferson** left to **James Madison** "my gold mounted walking staff of animal horn as a token of . . . cordial and affectionate friendship." Madison in turn left that cane and another, a walking staff from the timber of the U.S.S. *Constitution*, which had been presented to him by its Commander.

John Adams left no canes, but his son **John Quincy** left four, two of which were also made from the *Constitution*, clearly a whittled-down ship! Of the remaining two, one was ivory and the other of wood from an olive tree on Mount Olivet in Jerusalem.

Perhaps the biggest cane-fanciers were **Jackson** and **Benjamin Harrison**, with Jackson leaving his entire collection to his son, and Harrison bestowing upon his wife "the grand Army cane that I have used so long . . . and all other canes belonging to me," except for two canes of her choosing to be given to his brothers.

Tidbits & Trivia

AT LEAST HE WAS SPARED THAT

The tragedy of **Abraham Lincoln's** assassination produced a national grief never known before. It did, however, relieve the martyred President from facing an imminent family unpleasantness.

Mary Lincoln liked clothes. Mary Lincoln bought clothes. And more clothes. And then more clothes. She was, indeed, the First Lady of compulsive clothes buyers. At Lincoln's death, she had run up clothing bills amounting to $27,000. The day of domestic reckoning was near.

By his death, Lincoln's reputation for patience, tolerance, and understanding had been preserved. These magnificent qualities of his had been spared their ultimate test.

HOW WRONG HE WAS

Among other things, in his famous Gettysburg Address, **Abraham Lincoln** said, "The world will little note nor long remember what we say here."

IT WASN'T WHAT HE SAID

At the first Republican convention in Illinois, May 29, 1856, **Abe Lincoln** gave a great speech. The speech, given following the burning of a Kansas town by pro-slavery agitators, was so great nobody took any notes. They were totally wrapped up in Abe's denunciation of slavery and its evils. Nobody now knows what he said. It's called "Lincoln's Lost Speech."

If only we'd had TV.

THE PRESIDENTS

DON'T TOUCH IT!

Electric lights were installed in the White House in 1890 when the **Benjamin Harrisons** were residents.

This convenience would have been even more convenient for the Benjamin Harrisons if they hadn't been afraid to turn the lights on.

The Harrisons were quite conservative people. To them, electricity was something shocking, so the lights were turned on and off by servants.

LBJ ON BEAUTIFICATION

"I go upstairs and try to grab a nap in the afternoon," President **Lyndon B. Johnson** told his friends, "but Lady Bird and Laurence Rockefeller have a whole group of people in the next room talking about daffodils."

WHAT YOU SEE IS WHAT YOU GET

New furniture was in order after the British burned the White House during the War of 1812, and the **James Monroes** knew just what they wanted. They selected cherry chairs and a marble-topped table for the Oval Room, then sat back and waited for the French cabinetmaker to produce.

He did, and then some. Feeling their choice lacked the splendor due a head of state, the cabinetmaker gilded every piece. When the crates were opened in Washington, Mr. and Mrs. Monroe were astonished by the gleaming golden wood, but for diplomatic as well as practical reasons, made do.

Today those exquisite gilded furnishings are among the most prized White House antiques.

DID DOLLEY RUN OFF WITH GEORGE?

Legend has it that in 1814 when the British Army invaded Washington during the War of 1812, before fleeing the White House Dolley Madison cut the Gilbert Stuart portrait of **George Washington** from its frame and escaped from the Capital with the precious canvas.

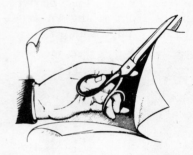

The matter is in some dispute, however. There are those who say that it was a servant who saved the painting, while Dolley took with her only a few silver spoons.

What do you think? Are you a "George" person or a "spoons" person?

Tidbits & Trivia

NINE HUNDRED NINETY-FOUR DUPES

In the 20th century, it has become the fashion for an administration to have a label. There was **Teddy Roosevelt's** "Square Deal," **Harry Truman's** "Fair Deal," **Woodrow Wilson's** "New Freedom," **John Kennedy's** "New Frontier," and **Lyndon Johnson's** "Great Society."

The most well-known of these, certainly the most enduring, was Franklin Roosevelt's "New Deal." The phrase was not created especially for the occasion. It had a source, and the source was a literary one, Mark Twain's *A Connecticut Yankee in King Arthur's Court.*

In the book, Chapter XIII (entitled Freemen) contains a passage in which Twain's storyteller says:

"And now here I was in a country where a right to say how the country should be governed was restricted to six persons in each thousand of its population . . . So to speak, I was to become a stockholder in a corporation where nine hundred and ninety-four of the members furnished all the money and did all the work, and the other six elected themselves a permanent board of direction and took all the dividends. It seemed to me that what the nine hundred ninety-four dupes needed was a new deal."

THIS IS THE WAY WE DRY OUR CLOTHES

The East Room of the White House has been the scene of many great receptions. The first reception held there, however, by Mrs. John Adams, was not for dignitaries. Abigail Adams wrote of the event to her daughter.

"We have not the least fence, yard, or other convenience without, and the great unfinished audience room, I make a drying room of, to hang the clothes in."

THEY DIDN'T SCARE HIM

Harry Truman shared what he called "hant" stories about the White House ghosts with his family, writing in 1946: "Now about the ghosts. I'm sure they're here and I'm not half so alarmed at meeting up with any of them as I am at having to meet the live nuts I have to see everyday."

Moreover, he figured he could learn something from them, adding: "I'm sure old Andy could give me some good advice and probably teach me some good swear words to use on Molotov and de Gaulle. And I am sure old Grover Cleveland could tell me some choice remarks to make to some political leaders. So I won't lock my doors or bar them either if any of the old coots in the pictures out in the hall want to come out of their frames for a friendly chat."

OH, TANNENBAUM!

The first White House Christmas tree was put up during **Benjamin Harrison's** administration in the upstairs Oval Room and decorated by the entire household.

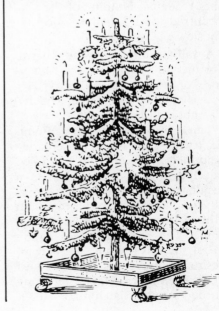

THE PRESIDENTS

"ON, BRAVE OLD ARMY TEAM"

"Going to West Point," wrote **Ulysses S. Grant** in his *Personal Memoirs,* "would give me the opportunity of visiting the two great cities of the continent, New York and Philadelphia. This was enough. When these places were visited I would have been glad to have had a steamboat or railroad collision, or any other accident happen, by which I might have received a temporary injury sufficient to make me ineligible, for a time, to enter the Academy. Nothing of the kind occurred, and I had to face the music . . .

"A military life held no charms for me, and I had not the faintest idea of staying in the army even if I should be graduated, which I did not expect."

When he arrived at West Point, he found that the representative who had appointed him had filled out the papers incorrectly. As a result, the rolls carried Grant as Ulysses Simpson Grant rather than Hiram Ulysses Grant, his real name. The new plebe was happy to let the error stand. He had no desire to make his life at West Point even more difficult by being burdened with the initials HUG.

KICKING THE HABIT

Twenty cigars daily were puffed by General **Ulysses S. Grant** who blamed the media (sound familiar?) for revealing his fondness for stogies after an important battle. The General explained that, "Many persons, thinking, no doubt, that tobacco was my chief solace, sent me boxes of the choicest brands . . . As many as ten thousand were soon received. I gave away all I could get rid of, but having such a quantity on hand I naturally smoked more than I would have done under ordinary circumstances and I have continued the habit ever since."

A PLAN FOR URBAN RENEWAL

Following his term as President, **Ulysses S. Grant** and Mrs. Grant took a world tour. He was particularly impressed with Venice but he did have one little suggestion. The city would be greatly improved if they drained it.

Tidbits & Trivia

LEADERSHIP BUT NO CHARISMA

In the presidential campaign of 1844, the Whig Party used the slogan, "Who the hell is James K. Polk?" This ridicule of the compromise Democratic candidate reflected Polk's lack of personal charm and national stature. Although reserved and lacking in the personal appeal usually associated with high office, he proved to be a tenacious, courageous, and capable President.

Polk was perhaps the only President to draw up a list of objectives at the beginning of his administration and accomplish them all (And in only a single term.)

Among the objectives was the Oregon boundary dispute, which had inspired the cry, "Fifty-four forty or fight!" by those who insisted the northern border of the Oregon Territory be established at that latitude, 54°40′. It was a rather colorful phrase and made good political fodder, but Polk had no expectation of getting land that far north and no intention of fighting for it. The matter was settled peaceably with Great Britain with the boundary established at 49°, where it is today.

Polk successfully directed the Mexican War and won vast new territories for the United States. When he retired to his Nashville home in 1849, however, he remained a remote and unloved figure.

AYE, A BONNIE TUNE

In 1844 Julia Tyler introduced the playing of "Hail to the Chief" to honor the President. Julia's Chief was husband **John Tyler.**

This Song of American Presidents is an old Gaelic melody adapted by a British composer for use in a musical drama about Scotland which was performed in England.

Sir Henry Rowland Bishop, composer and director of music at London's Covent Garden Theater, adapted the piece for use in a musical version of *The Lady of the Lake,* performed at the theater only briefly in 1811 and called *The Knight of Snowdoun.*

Bishop's lyric:

Hail to the Chief who in triumph
   advances!
Honored and blessed by the
   ever-green pine!
Long may the tree, in his banner
   that glances,
Flourish the shelter and grace
   of our line!

(Now it begins to get very Scottish)

Heaven send it happy dew,
Earth lend it sap to grow.
While every highland glen
Sends our shot back agen
"Roderigh Vich Alpine dhu, ho!
   ieroe!"

There were three more verses, but you get the general idea. Or the chief idea.

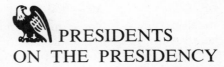

PRESIDENTS ON THE PRESIDENCY

Dignified slavery.
   Andrew Jackson

Toilsome and anxious probation.
   Martin Van Buren

THE PRESIDENTS

PLAY IT AGAIN, DOLLEY!

Even First Ladies can be sensitive to their age, no matter how public the record as to exactly how old they are.

Dolley Madison, in her eighties, was no exception. When a puzzled nephew at her birthday party said, "But Aunt Madison, that's the same age you were last year!" She replied, pleased, "So you remember, my little man!"

DEAR JAMES:

James Madison's first love was not Dolley. In 1782, while living at a boardinghouse in Philadelphia, the 31-year-old Madison fell in love with Catherine Floyd. Kitty lived at the boardinghouse with her father, William Floyd, who had been a signer of the Declaration of Independence. She was 15 and beautiful.

Madison and Kitty became engaged. Then they became disengaged. It seems that there was this young divinity student . . .

Kitty sent James a note announcing her change of heart. Perhaps in the 1780s there was a romantic significance to the method she used to seal the note. For those who care to speculate, Kitty sealed the note with rye bread dough.

THE REAL HOSTESS WITH THE MOSTES'

In the entire history of the Capital, Dolley Madison is far and away the city's most memorable hostess. But even after her husband's death, she continued as an important figure in Washington.

She returned to Washington at the age of 61 and reestablished herself in Washington society, where she reigned for twenty years and was honored by four more Presidents.

Although falling on hard times, with her famous pantry and fabulous wardrobe much restricted, she had as much charm as in her youth. Friends like Daniel Webster came calling, bringing a basket laden with groceries they con-

veniently "forgot" to fetch home. Others conspired to tactfully share other necessities of life with her, while still others worked toward getting Congress to purchase her husband's papers, so that she would have a small income.

While the elderly former First Lady struggled on the very brink of poverty, Congress at last acted and purchased the remaining Madison papers.

Able to eat, dress and entertain properly again, "Queen Dolley" graced one last administration, that of **Zachary Taylor**.

She even spent eight years in the Capital after her death, for she was buried in Washington, where she seemed to belong. Later, she was laid to rest beside her husband at Montpelier.

HALF A DOZEN

Want your son to be President? Name him James. Jimmy Carter is number six to be Number One. Prior to Jimmy Carter, the office was held by Jimmy Garfield, Jimmy Buchanan, Jimmy Polk, Jimmy Monroe, and Jimmy Madison.

DOLLEY'S HABIT

Dolley Madison took snuff.

Tidbits & Trivia

SCENE IN FRONT OF THE CONVENTION BUILDING DURING THE NOMINATION OF CANDIDATES, ON THE EVENING OF JUNE 5TH.

LOSING THE HARD WAY

On three occasions, the candidate receiving the greatest number of popular votes was the loser in a presidential election.

In 1824, **Andrew Jackson** received 153,544 votes and **John Quincy Adams** 108,740. Winner: Adams.

Reason: Since Jackson had not obtained a majority of electoral votes, the result had to be decided by the House of Representatives. Voting by states, with each state having one vote, the House elected Adams.

———

In 1876, Samuel Tilden had 4,300,590 votes and **Rutherford B. Hayes** 4,036,298. Tilden lost despite his popular majority of over 250,000.

Reason: 19 electoral votes were contested (Florida's 4, Louisiana's 8, and South Carolina's 7). In order to settle the dispute and award the 19 votes, Congress established a special electoral commission of five Senators, five Representatives, and five Justices of the Supreme Court to make a decision. It was understood that the commission consist of seven Republicans and seven Democrats plus one member who held independent views. Before the commission could meet, the independent member, a Supreme Court Justice, had to be replaced. The position was filled by another Justice, but this time, one who was Republican. Not surprisingly, the commission voted, eight to seven, to give the votes to Hayes, a Republican. This gave him a majority of the electoral votes, 185 to Tilden's 184.

It also won him a nickname: Rutherfraud.

———

In 1888, 5,540,309 people voted for **Grover Cleveland,** and 5,439,853 for **Benjamin Harrison,** who won the election.

Reason: Although Harrison had a smaller number of popular votes, he carried 20 states having a total of 233 electoral votes, while Cleveland carried 18 states with a total of 168.

———

Moral: The man who is voted most popular is not always the one most likely to succeed.

THE PRESIDENTS

SAD BUT TRUE

James Buchanan and Anne Coleman of Lancaster, Pennsylvania, were engaged. Anne's father, Robert, owned several iron forges and was one of America's first millionaires.

As soon as James and Anne were engaged, the rumor mills began to grind out the usual grist: he was marrying her for her money. Anne did not know whether to believe the stories, and her fiancé did not properly assure her that they were untrue. He was a busy and successful lawyer of 28 who frequently worked late at the office. Whether it was the rumors playing on her sensitive nature, or the fact that she didn't want to marry an office drudge, 23-year-old Anne broke the engagement.

She went to visit her sister in Philadelphia, presumably to recover from the broken engagement. She didn't recover. Instead, abruptly and unexpectedly, there at her sister's home, she died.

Suicide? Probably. Method? Probably something she swallowed. The attending physician attributed her death to an attack of what he called "convulsive hysteria." If so, it is possibly the only recorded case of this unique malady in the annals of medicine.

Buchanan wrote to Anne's father requesting permission to be a pallbearer at her funeral. The letter was returned unopened. For James Buchanan, a half-century of bachelorhood lay ahead.

SOME BEAUTY SECRET!

The control of advertising during the last century seems to have been several levels below nil.

According to one ad, the young and attractive Frances, wife of President **Grover Cleveland,** owed her beautiful complexion simply to "the use of arsenic, which can safely be taken and which can be procured from the New York doctor whose name appears in this advertisement."

For some reason, the ad failed to mention that a single application would last a lifetime or that the purchase price would be cheerfully refunded in the unlikely instance of the user expressing dissatisfaction.

PRESIDENTS ON THE PRESIDENCY

James Buchanan, just two years after taking office, bared his soul to Mrs. James K. Polk. "I am heartily tired of my position as President," he told her.

ONLY ONE...

Only one President, **James Buchanan**, never married.

Tidbits & Trivia

POLITICAL EXPERIENCE PRIOR TO THE PRESIDENCY, OR HOW I GOT MY JOB WITHOUT USING THE WANTAD SECTION

The route to the presidency is never short. It usually entails slowly working up the political ladder by taking on less rewarding positions of public office. For whatever it is worth to would-be high wire walkers, here is the record.

Foreign ministers:
J. Adams
Jefferson
Monroe
J. Q. Adams
Van Buren
W. H. Harrison
Buchanan

Positions in the Department of Treasury:
Arthur
Taft

Members of U.S. House of Representatives:
Madison
Jackson
W. H. Harrison
Tyler
Buchanan
Polk
Fillmore
Pierce
A. Johnson
Lincoln
Garfield
Hayes
McKinley
L. B. Johnson
Kennedy
Nixon
Ford

Members of U.S. Senate:
Monroe
Jackson
J. Q. Adams
Van Buren
W. H. Harrison
Tyler
Buchanan
Pierce
A. Johnson
Garfield (elected but did not serve)
Harding
Truman
L. B. Johnson
Kennedy
Nixon

State Governors:
Jefferson
Monroe
Van Buren
Tyler
Polk
A. Johnson
Hayes
Cleveland
McKinley
T. Roosevelt
Wilson
Coolidge
F. D. Roosevelt
Carter
Reagan

Territorial Governors:
Jackson
W. H. Harrison
Taft

Cabinet Members:
Jefferson
Madison
Monroe
J. Q. Adams
Van Buren
Buchanan
Grant
Taft
Hoover

Vice-Presidents:
J. Adams
Jefferson
Van Buren
Tyler
Fillmore
A. Johnson
Arthur
T. Roosevelt
Coolidge
Truman
L. B. Johnson
Nixon
Ford

THE PRESIDENTS

BOGERT & MECAMLY'S

John Tyler's second wife, Julia, a beautiful young woman, was 30 years younger than the President, (54 and 24 respectively when they were married.) She was called the Rose of Long Island. To locate her position more accurately, both geographically and socially, she had been Miss Julia Gardiner of Gardiner's Island.

A rose she may have been, but certainly no shrinking violet. In 1840 a newspaper advertisement for a department store appeared. It featured her picture and this comment by the lovely Julia:

"I'll purchase at Bogert & Mecamly's, No. 86 9th Avenue. Their Goods are Beautiful & Astonishingly Cheap."

4 times 11 are 44.

I bought this book at Francis' Store.

QUIET, PLEASE

Praying and fishing. Those are the only two presidential activities, according to **Herbert Hoover,** in which public and press respect the President's right of privacy. Everyone seems to concede that in both cases one must do it alone in order for the result to be successful.

4 times 12 are 48.

I wish that I could get some bait.

CAROLINE'S WHITE HOUSE

Mrs. Benjamin Harrison ran a tight domestic ship, and the White House was no exception. She swept it clean, literally from top to bottom, and in the process found enough china, broken and otherwise, to start the White House China Collection.

She also had some definite ideas about renovating the Executive Mansion, which included two vast greenhouse wings for the flowers, particularly orchids, which she loved.

Congress, however, in a rare moment of good sense, rejected the blueprints.

A YOUNG DUKE AND A DARK HORSE

The political term "dark horse" for an unlikely winner is, quite obviously, a racing term which has been applied to politics because of its relevance.

Perhaps the earliest appearance of the term in print was in a novel, *The Young Duke,* published in this country in 1832. The passage:

"A dark horse which had never been thought of, and which the careless St. James had never even observed in the list, rushed past the grandstand in sweeping triumph."

The author was a highly successful young novelist who later turned his talents to politics and ultimately became Prime Minister to Great Britain's Queen Victoria, Benjamin Disraeli. Speaking of dark horses . . .

6 times 11 are 66.

O see that Horse, how high he kicks.

Tidbits & Trivia

POPULAR FIGURE (BUT NOT WITH THE LADIES)

President and Mrs. Hayes (Rutherford and Lucy), the parents of eight children, celebrated their twenty-fifth wedding anniversary at the White House. The highlight of the event was the couple's renewal of their marriage vows.

At this Silver Wedding reception, the lovely Lucy Hayes wore the same dress in which she had been married.

6 times 10 are 60.
This pretty shawl will fix me.

NOW FOR YOUR HOMEWORK ASSIGNMENT

Abigail Powers was a teacher. One of her pupils was **Millard Fillmore.** Abigail taught Millard how to read and write.

Eliza McCardle was a teacher. One of her pupils was **Andrew Johnson.** Eliza taught Andrew how to read and write.

Millard married Abigail.

Andrew married Eliza.

Later they all went to the White House.

A man can learn a lot from his wife.

PASS GO AND MOVE DIRECTLY TO THE WHITE HOUSE

Vice President and Mrs. **Calvin Coolidge**, mindful of their modest means, had a small suite at Willard's Hotel in Washington while they served under President Harding.

Then Congress finally decided to appropriate money for an official vice presidential residence, but Mrs. Harding, who disliked "those Coolidges," and didn't want them to have so fine a house, used her considerable influence to kill the bill.

Ironically, "those Coolidges" moved into the White House itself, and Florence had to move out, when Warren Harding died before the end of his term.

HANDY FEATURE

A photograph of **James Buchanan** shows that he was a handsome and distinguished-looking man. If the photograph is one of Buchanan in a characteristic pose, his head will be cocked slightly. There was a reason for this. Buchanan was farsighted in one eye and nearsighted in the other, which is not a bad attribute for a politician.

NICE RECEPTION

John Kennedy was on the campaign trail. He stepped before the audience which had gathered to hear him speak. The audience applauded enthusiastically, and Kennedy expressed his appreciation. "As the cow said to the farmer," he smiled, "thanks for a warm hand on a cold morning."

DINNER AT THE WHITE HOUSE

On February 13, 1941, the young wife of a Congressman attended her first White House dinner, with **Eleanor** and **Franklin Roosevelt** as her hosts. She wrote:

"Tonight, I went to my first (will it be the last and only!?!) Dinner at the White House! Everything was managed with watchmaker's precision! Rep. Joe Casey was my dinner partner and very handsome and attractive. On the other side sat Sen. Sherman Minton. Was as far from the President as possible. The dinner was in honor of the Duchess of Luxembourg and her family — the President's houseguests. After dinner the ladies and Mrs. R. went to one drawing room and the men somewhere else. We had coffee and visited and Mrs. R. moved from group to group. Then we went upstairs and saw "Philadelphia Story" — big day!!"

The Congressman's wife was Mrs. Lyndon Johnson.

THE PRESIDENTS

PRESIDENTIAL RELIGIOUS AFFILIATION

Episcopalian (10)

Washington	Taylor
Madison	Pierce
Monroe	Arthur
W. H. Harrison	F. D. Roosevelt
Tyler	Ford

Presbyterian (7)

Jackson	B. Harrison
Polk	Wilson
Buchanan	Eisenhower
Cleveland	

Unitarian (4)

J. Adams	Fillmore
J. Q. Adams	Taft

Baptist (3)

Harding	Carter
Truman	

Disciples of Christ (3)

Garfield	Reagan
L. B. Johnson	

Dutch Reformed (2)

Van Buren	T. Roosevelt

Methodist (2)

Grant	McKinley

Society of Friends (Quaker) (2)

Hoover	Nixon

Congregationalist (1)

Coolidge

Roman Catholic (1)

Kennedy

No Affiliation (4)

Jefferson	A. Johnson
Lincoln	Hayes*

* Hayes at times attended Methodist church.

ETHICS OF PARENTS
By Eleanor Roosevelt

1. Furnish an example in living.
2. Stop preaching ethics and morals.
3. Have a knowledge of life's problems and an imagination.
4. Stop shielding your children and clipping their wings.
5. Allow your children to develop along their own lines.
6. Don't prevent self-reliance and initiative.
7. Have vision yourself and bigness of soul.

The next generation will take care of itself!

UPPITY INDEED

Mary Todd Lincoln came from a family so socially prominent that **Abe Lincoln** described it this way: "God spells His name with one d but the Todds spell theirs with two."

SIN

GRACE COOLIDGE: I'm sorry I missed the sermon. What was it about?

CALVIN COOLIDGE: Sin.

GRACE: What did the minister say about it?

CALVIN COOLIDGE: He was against it.

Tidbits & Trivia

WELCOME ADDITION, I THINK

Benjamin Harrison's grandson was a week old when his proud grandpa wrote about the baby's progress in a letter to Cousin Mag.

"As to the baby," he wrote, "I told his mother to say to him that if he would be patient until the snow is gone, we would all move out on the roof and give him the house."

HAPPY FATHER'S DAY

Once

William Henry Harrison, married once, was the father of ten children — six boys and four girls. This is the record for children born to a presidential marriage.

Twice

John Tyler, however, was married twice. He had three sons and five daughters with his first wife, five sons and two daughters with his second. In siring fifteen children, Tyler was the most fatherly of all the Presidents.

IT'S THINGS LIKE THIS THAT MAKE PEOPLE HAVE KIDS

Senator from Ohio and presidential aspirant, Robert Taft was once a little boy. He was a good little boy and seldom misbehaved, but on one such infrequent occasion he was about to be punished by his father.

"Are you going to spank me?" asked Robert.

"Yes," replied **William Howard Taft,** adding those well-worn words first uttered by a Stone Age parent, "and it's going to hurt me more than it hurts you."

"Then," said his son, "can I kiss you first?"

SOMETHING FOR THE LADIES

Woodrow Wilson, who had two sisters, three daughters and two wives must have been more sympathetic to the ladies than his predecessors, for he set precedent in appointing the first woman to a subcabinet post. She was Anne Abbott Adams, named Assistant Attorney General in 1920.

THAT'LL MAKE HIM BEHAVE

Kennedy children are brought up to win political elections. Two of Bobby's were in a department store one day. The girl was behaving like a lady, but her younger brother was behaving like a little boy in a department store, and people were turning to look. She spoke to him sharply. "Do be quiet. You're losing votes acting like this!"

ONLY ONE...

Only one President was the father of another President. **John Adams** was **John Quincy Adams'** father.

NO SINGLES ARE ADMITTED

No President was an only child.

THE BIRDS AND THE BEES

When Edith Roosevelt was asked by her stepdaughter, "How do little babies come?" Edith, already mother of three, responded: "God sends them. No one knows exactly how."

MORE PREACHERS' KIDS

First Ladies Abigail Adams and Caroline Harrison were both daughters of ministers.

THE PRESIDENTS

★ Washington's Headquarters

GEORGE WASHINGTON SLEPT HERE, AND HERE, AND HERE . . .

That **George Washington** visited a great many places is a matter of historical record. In 1932, on the bicentennial of Washington's birth *The George Washington Atlas* was published with 42 maps of George's journeys. It contains over 1,000 place names closely associated with Washington and is based on his diaries, journals and other writings.

As a surveyor and officer in the Virginia militia, George did get around, and as most-moving leader of the desperate American Army during the Revolution, Washington was able to elude the stronger British forces. After the war, as President he managed to put his feet up in quite a few quality places.

To fill a great informational void, we present the following as, we believe, the most definitive listing of George Washington's stop-overs. It includes all the places known to have been visited by the peripatetic Washington. Those sites which were Washington's headquarters during his military campaigns are designated by a special symbol.

At the end of each state listing, the reader will find a sampling of "other places" where Washington also stayed — the wayside inns, modest country houses and stately mansions. Because of space limitations our listing covering the social side cannot be complete; besides, not all George Washington's visits are a matter of record.

CONNECTICUT
Ashford
Berlin
 (Worthington)
Coventry
Danbury
Durham
East Hartford
Fairfield
Farmington
Greenwich
 (Horseneck)
Hartford
Harwinton
Lebanon
Litchfield
Mansfield
Middletown
Milford
New Haven
New London
New Preston
North Haven
Norwalk
Norwich
Old Lyme
 (Lyme)
Old Saybrook
 (Saybrook)
Pomfret
Stamford
Stratford
Suffield
Thompson
Wallingford
West Haven
Wethersfield
Windsor

DELAWARE
Christiana Bridge
Iron Hill
Naaman's Creek
Newark
New Castle
Newport ★
Red Lion
Stanton
Wilmington ★

Other Places
Buck Tavern

GEORGIA
Augusta
Hilltonia
McBean
Mulberry Grove
Savannah
Waynesborough

Other Places
Garnett's
Lambert's
Spencer's
Spinner's

MARYLAND
Allegany Grove
 (Gwin's)
Annapolis
Baltimore
Beltsville
Benedict
Bladensburg
Carrollsburg
Cedar Point
Charlestown
Chestertown
Clarksburg
 (Dowden's)
Conococheague
Cumberland
 (Will's Creek)
Down's Cross Roads
Elkridge Landing
Elkton
 (Head of Elk)
Frederick
 (Frederick Town)
Frostburg
 (Gillam's or Killam's)
Georgetown
 (Washington, D.C.)
Great Falls
Hancock
 (Barwick's)
Harford

Havre de Grace
Knowland's Ferry
 (Noland's Ferry)
Leeland Church
Little Falls
Little Meadows
Lower Cedar Point
Lower Ferry
Marlboro
Mason Springs
Nanjemoy
Nanjemoy Church
New Midway
 (Cookerly's Tavern)
Oakton
 (Mountain's)
Oldtown
 (Cresap's)
Perryville
 (Ferry House)
Piscataway
Port Tobacco
Queen Anne
Rockhall
Rockville
 (Owen's)
Savage
Seneca Falls
South River
Swan Point
Taneytown
Upper Marlboro
Vansville
 (Van Horne's Tavern)
Warwick
Washington, D.C.
Williamsburg
 (Rockville)
Williamsport

Other Places
Charles Polk's
Flint's
Gray's Hill
Keeptryst Furnace
Marshall Hall
Martin's Plantation
"Melwood,"
 Ignatius Digges'
"Mount Airy,"
 Benedict Calvert's
"Mount Lubentia," Bouchers'
Peter's Tavern
Rhode's Tavern
"Rose Hill," Dr. Brown's
Sutton's Tavern
"Warburton," William Digges'
Webster's Tavern
"Whitehall," Gov. Sharpe's
Widow Ramsay's

MASSACHUSETTS
Andover
Bellariki
Beverly
Boston
Bradford
Brookfield
Cambridge ★
Charlestown
Douglas
Haverhill
Holliston
Ipswich
Leicester
Lexington
Lynn
Malden
Marblehead
Marlborough
Medford
 (Mystick)
Menden
Milford
Needham
Newburyport
Palmer
Roxbury
Salem
Salisbury
Sherburn
Shrewsbury
Spencer
Springfield
Sudbury
Uxbridge
Watertown
Weston
Worcester

NEW HAMPSHIRE
Exeter
Greenland
Kingston
Kittery
Portsmouth

NEW JERSEY
Arcola
Basking Ridge
Belleville
Bernardsville
 (Vealtown)
Billingsport
Bordentown
Bound Brook ★
 (Middlebrook)
Burlington
Camden
Chatham ★
Closter
Cranbury ★
Elizabeth
 (Elizabeth Town)
Elizabethport
Englewood
Englishtown ★
Finderne
 (Van Veghten's Bridge)
Flemington
Fort Lee
Fredon
Freehold ★
 (Monmouth Court House)
Freneau
Gloucester Point
Green Village
Griggstown
Hackensack ★
Hackettstown
Hoboken
Hohokus
Hope
Hopewell
Jersey City
Kingston
Lambertville
 (Coryell's Ferry)
Landsdown
Lawrenceville
Leonia
Maidenhead
Manalapan
Maplewood
Montclair
Morristown ★
Mount Hope
Mount Vernon
Newark ★
New Brunswick ★
New Germantown
New Market ★
 (Quibbletown)
New Vernon
Newton
 (Sussex Court House)
Oakland
 (Pond Church)
Paramus ★
Parsippany
Passaic
 (Acquackanoc)
Paulus Hook
Perth Amboy
Pleasant Run
Pluckemin
Pompton ★
Pompton Plains ★
Preakness ★
Princeton
Rahway
Ramapo ★
Reading
Red Bank
 (Fort Mercer)
Ringwood
Rockaway
Rocky Hill ★
Sand Town
Sandy Hook
Scotch Plains
Somerville
Spotswood ★
Springfield ★
Stockton
 (Robinson's Ferry,
 Howell's Ferry)
Taylorsville
 (McKonkey's Ferry)

Teaneck ★
Totowa ★
Trenton
Trenton Ferry
Two Bridges ★
Union
 (Wadston, Wardiston)
Washington Corners
Whippany
Woodbridge

Other Places
Bullion's Tavern
Hopper House ★
Van Aulen's
 (near Oakland)

NEW YORK
Akin
 (Fort Johnson)
Albany
Amsterdam
Ballston Spa
Bedford
Bemis Heights
Brookhaven Township
 (Hart's Tavern)
Brooklyn
Canajoharie
Cherry Valley
Chester
Clarksville ★
 (Clarkstown)
Clinton
Cohoes
Continental Village
Cooperstown
Coram
Crown Point
Danube
Dobbs' Ferry ★
Duanesburg
Eastchester
Fishkill
Flatbush (Brooklyn)
Flushing (Queens)
Fonda
 (Caughnawaga)
Fort Edward
Fort Herkimer
Fort Hunter
Fort Plain
 (Fort Rensselaer)
Fort Washington (NYC)
Frankfort
Frogs Neck (Queens)
Glen Cove
 (Mosquito Cove)
Gravesend (Brooklyn)
Greenport
 (Sterling)
Harlem Heights
Haverstraw ★
Herkimer
 (Fort Dayton)
Hudson
Huntington
Hurley
Jamaica (Queens)
Kakiat ★
King's Bridge (Bronx)
King's Ferry ★
Kingsbury
Kingston
Lake George
 (Fort George)
Mamaroneck
Mechanicsville
Morrisania (NYC)
New Bridge
Newburgh ★
New Rochelle
Newtown
New Windsor ★
New York ★
North Castle
Oneida Castle
Oriskany
Oyster Bay
Palatine
Paris
Patterson
 (Fredericksburg)
Peekskill ★
Phillipsburg ★
Poughkeepsie ★
Queensbury
 (near Glens Falls)
Rome

Tidbits & Trivia

Rosendale
Rye
Salt Springville
Saratoga Springs
 (High Rock Springs)
Sauquoit
Schenectady
Schuylerville
 (Old Saratoga)
Setauket
 (Setakit)
Sing Sing
Sloatsburg ★
Smithtown
Sneden's Landing
Southfields ★
 (Galloway's in
 the Clove)
South Hempstead
Springfield
Stillwater
Stone Ridge
 (Marbletown)
Stony Point ★
Suffern ★
 (Suffern's Tavern)
Tappan ★
 (Orangetown)
Tarrytown ★
Ticonderoga
Troy
Utica
 (Old Fort Schuyler)
Utrich
 (New Utrich)
Verplanck's Point
Warwick
West Point ★
White Plains ★
Wilton
Yonkers

Other Places
Appleby's ★
Nolan's Hotel
Robinson House
Smith's Tavern ★
Tippett's Hill
Van Cortlandt's Mansion

NORTH CAROLINA
Charlotte
Greenville
Guilford
Halifax
New Bern
Salem

Salisbury
Tarboro
Trenton
Wilmington

Other Places
"Belvidere,"
 Col. Benjamin Smith's
Crown Point Inn
Everett's
Foy's
Gatewood's
Young's

OHIO
Little Hocking
Long Reach
Mingo Junction
 (Mingo Town)

PENNSYLVANIA
Aliquippa
Barren Hill
Bedford
 (Raystown)
Bethlehem
 (Bethelem)
Bristol
Canonsburg
 (Cannon's)
Carlisle
Chadds Ford ★
Chambersburg
Chester
Chester Springs
 (Yellow Springs)
Confluence
 (Turkey Foot)
Conshohocken
Croghan's
Cussawago
Darby ★
Doylestown
Easton
Economy
 (Logs Town)
Evansburg
Farmington
Fort Necessity
Frankford
Franklin
 (Venango)
Germantown ★
Great Swamp
Greencastle
Gulf Mill ★

Hanover
Harrisburg
Hatboro
 (Crooked Billet Tavern)
Hazel Dell
 (Murdering Town)
Hummelstown
Kinkade's Ferry
Lancaster
Lebanon
Leiperville
Limerick Square
Ligonier
 (Loyal Hanna)
Lionville
 (Red Lion Tavern)
Littlestown
Malin Hall ★
Marcus Hook
McKees Rocks
Monongahela
 (Devore's Ferry)
Morrisville ★
Mount Braddock
Myerstown
New London
Newtown ★
Neshaminy Camp ★
Nicetown
Norristown
 (Swede's Ford)
Paoli
 (Warren)
Parker's Ford
Perryopolis
 (Simpson's)
Philadelphia ★
Pittsburgh
 (Fort Duquesne,
 Fort Pitt)
Pottstown
Quitipohilla Canal
Reading
Reading Furnace ★
Rock Fort
Salt Lick
Sanatoga ★
 (Pottsgrove)
Schuylkill Fells ★
Schwenksville ★
 (Pennybacker's Mill)
Shippensburg
Skippack ★
Somerfield
 (Great Crossing)
Squaw's Fort
Stewart's Crossing

Towamencin ★
Trappe
Uniontown
 (Beason Town)
Valley Forge ★
Warwick
Waterford
 (Fort Le Boeuf)
White Marsh ★
Whitepain ★
 (Whitpain)
Womelsdorf
Worcester ★
 (Peter Wentz's)
Wright's Ferry
York
 (York Town)

Other Places
Buck's Tavern
Daugherty's
Frazier's
Keith's ★
Jane Moore's
Thompson's Tavern
White Horse Tavern
Widow Miers'

RHODE ISLAND
Bristol
Newport
Providence
South Kingston
Warren
Westerly

SOUTH CAROLINA
Ashley River Bridge
Camden
Charleston
Columbia
Fort Johnson
Fort Moultrie
Georgetown
Granby
Haddrel's Point
Lynch's Ferry
Manigault's
Odom's
Pokitellico
Purisburgh
Sandy Hill

Other Places
Cochran's
Dr. Flagg's

Gov. Pinckney's
 Country Seat
Holliday's Tavern
James Ingram's
Judge Bee's
Judge Hayward's
Major Crawford's
Mrs. Horry's
Sutton's

VIRGINIA
Accotink
Alexandria
 (Belhaven)
Andersons Bridge
Aquia
Auburn
Aylett
Bacon's Fort
Bowler's
Bowling Green
Boyd's Hole
Burwell's Ferry
Cameron
Capahosic
Cartersville
Centreville
 (Newgate)
Chamberlayne's Ferry
Charlotte Court House
Claiborne's Ferry
Colchester
Cole's Ford
Culpeper
Cumberland
Danzie's Ferry
Dinwiddie
Dix Ferry
Dumfries
Fairfax
Falmouth
Ferry Landing
Four Mile Run
Fredericksburg
Gloucester
Great Bridge
Great Falls
Green Spring
Hampden Sidney
 (Prince Edward C.H.)
Hampton
Hanover
Hoe's Ferry
Hog Island Ferry
Keysville
 (Vestal's Gap)
King William

Knowland's Ferry
Layton's Ferry
Leedstown
Leesburg
Luney's Ferry
Manchester
Mount Vernon
New Castle
New Kent
Nomini Grove
Norfolk
 (Berkley)
Oak Grove
Occoquan
Payne's Church
 (New Church)
Petersburg
Peytonsburg
 (Halifax Old Town)
Piscataway Ferry
Pohick Church
Port Conway
Port Royal
Portsmouth
Rappahannock Farm
Richmond
Saint Peter's Church
Sheridan's Point
Shirley Duke
Smithfield
Southall's
Southern's Ferry
Stafford
Staunton
 (Augusta Court House)
Stephens Town
Suffolk
Swift Run Gap
Tappahannock
 (Hobb's Hole)
Trebell's
Urbanna
Wakefield
 (Bridges Creek)
Washington's Mill
Westover
West Point
Winchester
 (Frederick Town)
Williamsburg ★
Williams' Ferry
Yorktown

Other Places
"Abingdon," John
 Parke Custis'
Alexander Spotswood's

"Ampthill," Archibald
 Cary's
Ashby's Ferry
"Belvoir," George
 William Fairfax's
"Bushfield," John
 Augustine Washington's
Chiswel's Ordinary
"Eagle's Nest,"
 Nathaniel Harrison's
"Greenway Court,"
 Lord Fairfax's
"Gunston Hall,"
 George Mason's
Henry Lee's
Mrs. Jordan's
Moore's Tavern
"Mount Eagle," Bryan
 Fairfax's
"Nomini Hall," Robert
 Carter's
Pickett's Ordinary
Snead's Ordinary
Treadway's
Watt's Ordinary
Widow Beringer's
Widow Paine's
Widow Yearly's
"Wilton,"
 Mrs. Randolph's

WEST VIRGINIA
Berkeley Springs
 (Bath, Warm Springs)
Bunker Hill
 (Morgan's)
Capon Bridge
 (Edwards Fort)
Charles Town
Happy Retreat
Harewood
Harpers Ferry
Okonoko
Parkersburg
Point Pleasant
Reeve's Mill
Romney
Wheeling Indian Town

Other Places
Enoch's
Henry Van Meter's
Peter Casey's

Overseas
Barbados

THE PRESIDENTS

ALICE ON JUST ABOUT EVERYONE

Alice Roosevelt Longworth, TR's daughter, was quite outspoken about the occupants of the White House or anyone within striking distance of her barbed tongue. She provided Washington correspondents with a great many quotable quotes. Here are a few.

ALICE ON WARREN

"Harding was not a bad man," said Alice. "He was just a slob."

ALICE ON HERBERT

T.R.'s daughter, a staunch Republican, supported Hoover for reelection when interviewed by a member of the press. But to friends, she had this to say, "The Hoover Vacuum Cleaner is more exciting than the President. But of course, it's electric."

ALICE ON FRANKLIN

Alice was equally blunt about her distant cousin, FDR.

"He was the kind of boy whom you invited to the dance but not the dinner," she said. "A good little mother's boy whose friends were dull. Who belonged to the minor clubs and who never was at the really good parties."

ALICE ON IKE

"Eisenhower," murmured Alice. "A nice boob."

ALICE ON JERRY

"I've never met him," said Alice when Jerry Ford became President. "But he's from Ohio, and they turn out Jerry Fords by the bale!"

BECAUSE

Thomas E. Dewey ran for President against **Franklin D. Roosevelt** in 1944 and lost.

Dewey ran for President again in 1948, this time against **Harry Truman,** and lost again.

Alice Longworth, **Teddy Roosevelt's** daughter and a kind of Washington monument in her own right, commented on Dewey's lack of popular appeal.

"How can you vote for a man," she asked, "who looks like the bridegroom on a wedding cake?"

ALICE ON ELEANOR

T.R.'s daughter, Alice Roosevelt Longworth did not have many good things to say about her cousin Eleanor. As a child, she found Eleanor "full of duty, never very gay, a frightful bore for the more frivolous people like ourselves." As an adult commenting on the Franklin Roosevelt-Lucy Mercer romance, she said, "He deserved a good time. He was married to Eleanor." "Princess" Alice did pay Eleanor one compliment on her conduct as wife of the Assistant Secretary of the Navy newly arrived on the Washington scene: "She did her job better than most," Alice admitted.

At another time she had this to say about her cousin:

"As far as I'm concerned, Eleanor really came into her own *after* Franklin died. Before, she was too noble — a person who had gone down in one coal mine too many."

ALICE ON THE PRESS

"The trouble with reporters," said T.R.'s daughter, "is that they expect me to wear a halo, and I only wear a hat!"

ALICE ON ALICE

"A combination of Scarlett O'-Hara and Whistler's Mother."

ALICE IN WONDERLAND

More than half a century after her fairy-tale White House wedding, Alice Roosevelt Longworth, T.R.'s daughter, commented on the long list of wedding gifts from heads of state published in the press. "I only wish I'd gotten all those things they said I got," she said.

Tidbits & Trivia

ALICE ON WATERGATE

Here's another of Alice Roosevelt Longworth's comments on the Washington scene.

"I'll remember Watergate as good, unclean fun."

ALICE ON NIXON

"Dick is a weaker man than I thought him. Weak, weak, weak! Kennedy *never* would have shilly-shallied the way Nixon is doing. The tapes should have been destroyed and enough of this nonsense!"

TAKE YOUR CHOICE

The novelist Owen Wister, a friend of **Theodore Roosevelt,** visited the President at the White House often. During one of these visits, the two friends were having a quiet chat which was being continually interrupted by the President's high-spirited eldest daughter, Alice.

"Theodore," said Wister, "isn't there anything you can do to control Alice?"

"I can do one of two things," Roosevelt replied. "I can either be President of the United States or I can control Alice. I cannot possibly do both."

WAS HE TALKING NATURE OR POLITICS?

The November 1913 issue of *Boys' Life* magazine advertised on its cover a feature story by **Theodore Roosevelt** entitled, "About Man Eating Lions."

TEDDY BEAR

The Teddy Bear was created and named in honor of President **Teddy Roosevelt.** T. R.'s refusal to shoot a bear cub while hunting inspired a political cartoon which in turn triggered the manufacture of Teddy Bears.

WILL THE REAL FALL-GUY PLEASE STAND UP?

He may just have been carrying on a political tradition, but Albert Fall, Harding's Secretary of the Interior, was the first to get caught at it when he became the first cabinet official to be convicted of a crime October 25, 1929.

The charge? Bribery.

Years later, in the wake of Watergate and half a century of other major and minor political scandals, Alice Roosevelt Longworth recalled, "Forty or fifty years ago I gave a party for a great friend of ours — Albert Fall. Meanwhile, his pockets were rustling with one hundred dollar bills. I'm afraid I keep up my associations whether people are criminal or not. I'm very careless about that."

BROUGHT DOWN TO EARTH

Quentin Roosevelt was walking on stilts in a White House flower bed.

"Quentin, get out of there," called his father.

From his elevated position, Son Quentin looked down at Father Teddy. "I don't see what good it does *me,*" grumbled Quentin, "for *you* to be President."

ABOUT CHURCH AND STATE

Teddy Roosevelt had no problems with the separation between the two. He just said the White House was "A Bully Pulpit!"

THE PRESIDENTS

DON'T BACK ZACH

Margaret Taylor's prayers included a request that her husband, Zachary, not be nominated for the presidency. To others she denounced the nomination as "a plot to deprive her of his society and shorten his life."

Taylor was nominated.

Taylor was elected.

After less than a year and a half in office, Taylor died.

Sorry about that, Margaret.

LOST YOUTH

Following the assassination of **John F. Kennedy,** Washington newspaper columnist Mary McGory said in shock and dismay to Daniel Moynihan, "We'll never laugh again."

Moynihan, Assistant Secretary of Labor, a man close to Kennedy, replied sadly, "Heavens, Mary, we'll laugh again. It's just that we'll never be young again."

THAT MOMENT IN AIR FORCE ONE

United States District Judge Sarah Hughes had the unique and solemn responsibility of administering the presidential oath to **Lyndon Johnson** in the cabin of Air Force *One,* following **John Kennedy's** assassination.

She was the only woman ever to administer the oath.

It was a day on which the sexes were clearly, shatteringly equal.

ZEROING IN — OR OUT

Ever since 1840, every President first elected in a year ending with a zero has died in office. Only two Chief Executives, Thomas Jefferson, elected in 1800, and James Monroe, elected in 1820, have escaped this cruel twist — or fickle finger — of fate.

The victims include: William Henry Harrison, elected in 1840 (dead of pneumonia just a month afterward); Abraham Lincoln, elected in 1860, reelected four years later (assassinated shortly thereafter); James A. Garfield, elected in 1880 (assassinated six months after taking office); William McKinley, elected in 1900 (assassinated six months after taking office); Warren G. Harding, elected in 1920 (dead of mysterious causes three years later); Franklin D. Roosevelt, elected in 1940 for the third time (dead of natural causes April 1945 after reelection for a fourth time); and

John F. Kennedy, elected in 1960 (assassinated in 1963).

Candidates for the presidency in 1960 were asked about the "zero factor" and its effect on their future presidential aspirations. Replying by letter, Senator John F. Kennedy wrote:

"The historical curiosity . . . is indeed thought-provoking . . . I feel that the future will have to necessarily answer this for itself — both as to my aspirations and my fate should I have the privilege of occupying the White House.

"On face value, I daresay, should anyone take this phenomenon to heart . . . anyone, that is, who aspires to change his address to 1600 Pennsylvania Ave. . . . that most probably the landlord would be left with a 'For Rent' sign hanging on the gate-house door."

As for the election of 1980, the attempt on Ronald Reagan's life one month after his taking office seems already too scary.

Tidbits & Trivia

YOU DON'T GET A CANAL BY GOING THROUGH CHANNELS

In 1902, Panama was a province of Colombia, and it was with the Colombian government that **Theodore Roosevelt** had to deal for the rights to dig a canal across the Panamanian isthmus. But dealing with Colombia was not easy.

As TR himself put it, "You could no more make an agreement with the Colombian rulers than you could nail currant jelly to the wall."

With a little encouragement from Guess Who, Panama revolted successfully and became an independent country. Its independence was officially recognized by the United States in exactly three days, and a canal treaty for the rights to begin work was signed 12 days later. (If you are wondering what took Teddy so long, remember he didn't speak the language.)

End of Part I. Beginning of Part II. Work on canal begins. Work on canal progresses. Theodore Roosevelt speaks:

"I am interested in the Panama Canal because I started it. If I had followed conservative conventional methods, I should have submitted a dignified state paper of approximately 200 pages to the Congress and the debate would have been going on yet, and while the debate goes on, the Canal does also."

CAL MEETS THE BABE

Calvin Coolidge went to the ball game one warm day. The Washington Senators were playing the New York Yankees.

Before the game, the President met the players, among whom was the immortal Babe Ruth.

It was Ruth's turn to be introduced. Knowing he had little in common with the President of the United States, and equally little to talk about, the Babe decided on a neutral, time-tested topic of conversation: the weather.

He extended his hand. "Hot as hell, ain't it, Prez," he remarked.

THAT'S JUST HOW IT IS

The only man in the nation's history to serve as President who hadn't been elected to that office or to that of the vice-presidency, but was appointed V.P. and succeeded to the top spot when **Nixon** resigned, may have known more about losing the job more than any other candidate.

When he lost the election that would have made him President in his own right, **Gerald R. Ford** said, "No one likes to lose. But it's not the end of the world."

AND MAMA MAKES THREE

The first President's mother to share the White House with her son and daughter-in-law was Eliza Ballou Garfield, mother of President **James Garfield.**

Unfortunately, he was assassinated barely six months after taking office, so we have no way of knowing how the arrangement suited James's wife, Lucretia.

THE FIRST

The first President to open the baseball season was **William Howard Taft,** who threw out the first ball prior to the game between Washington and the Philadelphia Athletics at the start of the 1910 season.

SLIGHTLY AMBIGUOUS

Woodrow Wilson had suffered a stroke. His unsuccessful efforts to win the support of the Senate and the American people for his peace treaty had sapped his strength and led to his physical collapse.

A delegation of Senators visited the sick President. "We've all been praying for you," one of them said.

Wilson's mind had not been affected by the stroke, nor had his sense of humor.

"Which way, Senator?" he asked.

THE PRESIDENTS

WATCHING THEIR WEIGHT

In a constant battle to keep trim, Richard Nixon lunched on cottage cheese and ketchup. Lyndon Johnson preferred low-calorie tapioca pudding.

Neither diet has caught on.

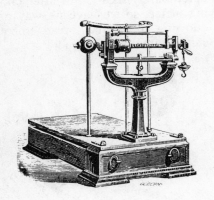

JACKIE ON LADY BIRD JOHNSON

"Lady Bird would walk on cut glass for her husband."

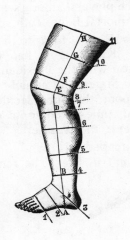

GOOD ADVICE, BUT DID SHE TAKE IT?

Florence Harding had a lot to say about a lot of things, but she was especially outspoken about how to keep a man. "Always have an icebox full of food, and never let him travel without you."

FRANKLY SPEAKING

About the nicest thing Congress could do to show respect for First Ladies was to grant them the franking privilege, which entitled them to free postal service, something that might not have been worth much when it was first extended to Martha Washington on April 3, 1800, "for and during her life."

The same privilege today, considering the cost of first-class mail, is worth quite a bit!

ANNIVERSARY WALTZ

Four presidential couples celebrated golden wedding anniversaries. Three of the four marriages lasted even longer.

John and Abigail **Adams** — 54 years
John Quincy and Louisa **Adams** — 50 years
Harry and Bess **Truman** — 53 years
Dwight and Mamie **Eisenhower** — 52 years

JOHNSON AND JOHNSON

When Lady Bird Johnson and her entourage traveled through Pennsylvania by car, they decided to stop like other travelers at Howard Johnson's restaurant, taking the precaution of calling ahead for a table of 28 to accommodate all the press and Secret Service personnel with them.

After lunch, a reporter asked a waitress, "How did you feel serving the First Lady?"

"First Lady!" squealed the waitress. "Oh my God, thank goodness I didn't know it. I would have fainted dead away. I thought it was Mrs. Howard Johnson — that was bad enough."

Tidbits & Trivia

FRANCES THE FIRST

Frances Perkins, appointed by **Franklin Roosevelt** to the position of Secretary of Labor in 1933, was the first woman cabinet officer. She held the post until 1945.

When asked if being a woman was a handicap, she replied, "Only in climbing trees."

HE MADE HIS POINT

Following World War I, **Woodrow Wilson's** program for lasting peace was embodied in a covenant containing his Fourteen Points. He presented this to the Allied leaders.

Georges Clemenceau, French premier, whose opinion of the United States was that it was the only country in the history of the world that had gone from barbarism to decline without the intervening step of civilization, had a few words to say on the Fourteen Points as well.

"God Almighty gave us Ten Commandments," said Clemenceau, "and we broke those. Now we have Wilson who gives us Fourteen."

SMILIN' CAL STRIKES AGAIN

The only live President to be honored with his image on a coin was **Calvin Coolidge**, who appeared with George Washington on the 1926 Sesquicentennial half-dollar.

CAPITAL! CAPITAL!

The only foreign country having a capital named for an American President is Liberia. The President was **James Monroe** and the city, Monrovia.

Fact: Liberia, a West African nation founded in 1822, was the very first independent African republic.

Fact: It was founded and financed largely through the efforts of the American Colonization Society to provide a home for free blacks and captured slaves.

Fact: The efforts of the Society were strongly supported and subsidized by the United States Government and its President, James Monroe, hence the naming of the Liberian capital in his honor.

Fact: James Monroe, whose name continues to be so honored by the first free African nation, was a slave-owner.

TOM . . . AS IN TOMATO

Thomas Jefferson was the first President to grow a tomato. In fact he was the first person in North America to grow a tomato. At the time, most people thought that tomatoes were poisonous. But Tom Jefferson never was most people.

SOMETIMES YOU CAN'T PLEASE ANYBODY

Secretary of State William H. Seward was the man primarily responsible for the purchase of Alaska from Russia for $7,200,000. Although this amounted to less than two cents an acre, perhaps the American people were more economy-minded than they are today. They considered the purchase an extravagant foolishness and referred to Alaska as "Seward's Folly."

Andrew Johnson was President at the time and he, too, came in for his share of the "glory." Those who didn't call it "Seward's Folly" referred to Alaska as "Andy Johnson's Polar Bear Garden."

THE PRESIDENTS

A TREND HERE?

Six of the last ten Presidents were born west of the Mississippi River.

Only two Presidents were born in large cities, **William Taft** and **Teddy Roosevelt**.

PARTING SHOTS

The last words of a few Presidents just before death were overheard and recorded for posterity:

George Washington — "Doctor, I die hard, but I am not afraid to go."

John Quincy Adams — "This is the last of earth! I am content."

Theodore Roosevelt — "Please put out the lights."

Franklin Delano Roosevelt — "I have a terrific headache."

WHERE THERE WASN'T A WILL

Four Presidents, **Lincoln, Andrew Johnson, Grant** and **Garfield**, died without a will, leaving, in each case, a widow and one or more children at the mercy of the laws of the state in which they had lived.

It seems incredible that these Chief Executives of the United States, and especially Lincoln, an attorney, failed in this simple obligation to their families. Or maybe they just had more confidence in the Government's ability to tax and distribute equitably!

President	Birthplace	Place of Burial
1. Washington	Wakefield, Va.	Mount Vernon, Va.
2. J. Adams	Braintree, Mass.	Quincy, Mass.
3. Jefferson	Albemarle Co., Va.	Monticello, Va.
4. Madison	Port Conway, Va.	Montpelier, Va.
5. Monroe	Westmoreland Co., Va.	Richmond, Va.
6. J. Q. Adams	Braintree, Mass.	Quincy, Mass.
7. Jackson	Waxhaw, S. C.	Hermitage, Tenn.
8. Van Buren	Kinderhook, N. Y.	Kinderhook, N. Y.
9. W. H. Harrison	Berkeley, Va.	North Bend, Ohio
10. Tyler	Greenway, Va.	Richmond, Va.
11. Polk	near Pineville, N. C.	Nashville, Tenn.
12. Taylor	Orange Co., Va.	near Louisville, Ky.
13. Fillmore	Locke, N. Y.	Buffalo, N. Y.
14. Pierce	Hillsboro, N. H.	Concord, N. H.
15. Buchanan	Franklin Co., Pa.	Lancaster, Pa.
16. Lincoln	Hardin Co., Ky.	Springfield, Ill.
17. A. Johnson	Raleigh, N. C.	Greeneville, Tenn.
18. Grant	Point Pleasant, Ohio	New York, N. Y.
19. Hayes	Delaware, Ohio	Fremont, Ohio
20. Garfield	Orange, Ohio	Cleveland, Ohio
21. Arthur	Fairfield, Vt.	Albany, N. Y.
22 & 24. Cleveland	Caldwell, N. J.	Princeton, N. J.
23. B. Harrison	North Bend, Ohio	Indianapolis, Ind.
25. McKinley	Niles, Ohio	Canton, Ohio
26. T. Roosevelt	New York, N. Y.	Oyster Bay, N. Y.
27. Taft	Cincinnati, Ohio	Arlington, Va.
28. Wilson	Staunton, Va.	Washington, D. C.
29. Harding	Blooming Grove, Ohio	Marion, Ohio
30. Coolidge	Plymouth, Vt.	Plymouth, Vt.
31. Hoover	West Branch, Iowa	West Branch, Iowa
32. F. D. Roosevelt	Hyde Park, N. Y.	Hyde Park, N. Y.
33. Truman	Lamar, Mo.	Independence, Mo.
34. Eisenhower	Denison, Texas	Abilene, Kans.
35. Kennedy	Brookline, Mass.	Arlington, Va.
36. L. Johnson	near Stonewall, Texas	near Stonewall, Texas
37. Nixon	Yorba Linda, Calif.	—
38. Ford	Omaha, Nebr.	—
39. Carter	Plains, Ga.	—
40. Reagan	Tampico, Ill.	

HE KEPT IT SHORT

The shortest and simplest presidential will was that written by Calvin Coolidge. It supports the testator's well-known reputation for taciturnity and succinct expression. It reads as follows:

"The White House" Washington
*Not unmindful of my son John, I give all my estate both real and personal to my wife Grace Coolidge, in fee simple — Home at Washington, District of Columbia this twentieth day December,*A.D. *nineteen hundred and twenty six.*

Calvin Coolidge

Tidbits & Trivia

BIRTHPLACES and PLACES OF BURIAL

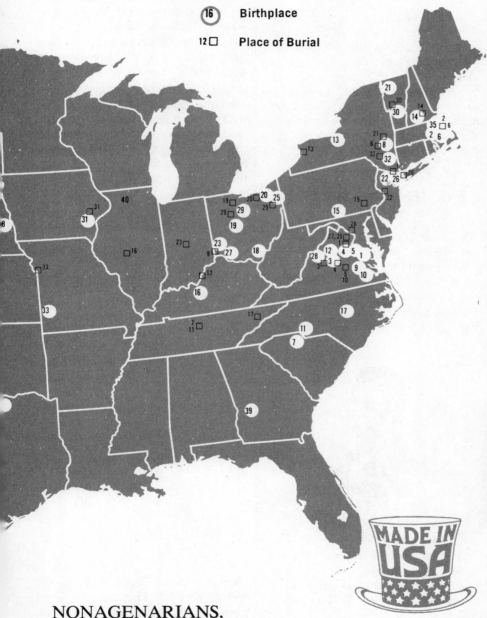

- ⑯ Birthplace
- 12☐ Place of Burial

MADE IN USA

NONAGENARIANS, OCTOGENARIANS

Two Presidents lived past their 90th birthdays.

John Adams — 90 years, 247 days

Herbert Hoover — 90 years, 71 days

Four lived past their 80th:

Jefferson — 83 years, 82 days

Madison — 85 years, 104 days

John Quincy Adams — 80 years, 227 days

Truman — 88 years, 232 days

JOHN SCOTT HARRISON: NOT JUST ANY BODY

The only man in the history of the United States to be the son of one President and the father of another was John Scott Harrison, son of **William Henry Harrison** and father of **Benjamin Harrison.** He, himself, was a two-term Congressman. But hold on! There's more!

John Scott died peacefully enough, at the age of 73, and was properly interred. Then, a short time after his burial, he was missing.

A frantic search for him finally was successful, in an unpleasant sort of way. J. S. was discovered carefully hidden in the dissecting room of the Ohio Medical College, about to make a posthumous contribution to medical education.

Supplying medical schools with cadavers for student use was a common practice in 1878, and a lucrative business as well, but there were risks. One really ought

to ascertain that the body provided was not that of a man who had been the son of a President and the father of a prospective one.

John Scott Harrison's final participation in the passing parade was to inspire great national indignation over what had happened to him. The result was the enactment of legislation that made the penalty for bodynapping very, **very** severe.

THE PRESIDENTS

SOMEBODY CHECK THOSE FILES

It seems ridiculous, but there it is. The Number One Presidential Executive Order in the files of the Department of State is dated October 20, 1862, and is signed by **Abraham Lincoln**. Either no executive orders were issued by earlier Chief Executives or it took almost one hundred years to get the files organized.

·····●●●●·····

BAR TENDER ADMITTED TO BAR

Abraham Lincoln took out a saloon license to enable him to dispense spirits at the establishment of Berry and Lincoln in Springfield, Illinois, in 1833.

He was eventually admitted to the bar, legal that is, March 1, 1837.

BUT WHAT DID THE *TIMES* SAY ABOUT IT?

A number of contemporary newspapers reviewed **Lincoln's** Gettysburg Address. One of these was the Chicago *Times*. The *Times* had this to say:

"The cheek of every American must tingle with shame as he reads the silly, flat and dish-watery utterances of the man who has been pointed out to intelligent foreigners as the President of the United States."

NOTEWORTHY PRIZE

On April 10, 1865, Washington crowds, overjoyed at the news of Robert E. Lee's surrender, surged around the White House, cheering and calling for the President to come out and make a speech.

Abraham Lincoln appeared, quieted the throng, and promised to make a few remarks. But first, he said, turning toward the members of a band which was at the scene, he had a request. He would like the band to play "Dixie."

"Dixie?" The Confederate song? Why "Dixie?" The crowd stirred restlessly. Was this another one of Lincoln's jokes?

" 'Dixie,' " he said, "is one of the best tunes I have ever heard, and now we have captured it."

A mighty cheer went up from the crowd and the band played "Dixie."

Tidbits & Trivia

"... AND THE PURSUIT OF HAPPINESS."

George Washington was a man who worked hard. From the grave mien exhibited in his portraits, it would appear that George never had any fun. But he did.

Here is a list of things that he enjoyed:

1. Raffles and lotteries
2. Playing cards (He kept careful written records of his winnings and losses.)
3. Fox hunting
4. Duck hunting
5. Fishing
6. Cockfighting
7. Horse racing (At the Annapolis track)
8. Boat racing
9. Dancing (He compared it to war and called it "the gentler conflict.")
10. Going to the theater (*School for Scandal*, *Julius Caesar*, and *Hamlet* were among the hits he attended, but there were turkeys as well.)
11. Attending concerts
12. Visiting and entertaining
13. Going to barbecues
14. Raising dogs

He was an enthusiastic breeder of hounds, and the names he gave them provide some insight into his character. Among the males were Drunkard, Tippler, Trueman, and Tarter. The bitches included Lady, Duchess, Truelove, and Sweetlips.

Anyone making a list of our more straitlaced presidents should not include George.

THAT'S WHAT YOU GET FOR YOUR $20

Harry Truman wanted to build a porch on the White House. The funds were available and the porch was added. No problem.

Oh, yes. One problem. On the back of the $20 bill there appears a view of the White House. A new plate had to be engraved to show the new porch.

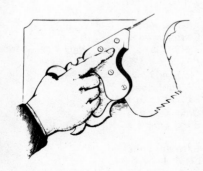

FIRST LADIES OF THE CONFEDERACY

Knox Taylor, daughter of President **Zachary Taylor**, was the bride of Jefferson Davis, who later became President of the Confederate States of America. Davis remained a widower for many years after her untimely death. Zachary Taylor always considered Jefferson Davis as family, even after his remarriage.

Jefferson Davis's second wife, Varina, was close to the Taylors, but her closest friendship was even more unusual. She and Julia Grant, widow of the former Union General and President, spent their twilight years as friends and neighbors in New York. It was a remarkable association: elderly widows of the men who stood as symbols of the North and South, living examples of love and affection, forgiveness and peace.

THE FIRST

The first President born an American citizen, not a British subject, was **Martin Van Buren.**

THAT'S NOT SO FUNNY

James K. Polk, an outstanding President, was a man so devoid of humor that the funniest thing he ever did was to have a gallstone operation without anesthesia at the age of 17 in the backwoods of Kentucky.

THE PRESIDENTS

PLEASE NAME IT AFTER ME

Washington is the only American state which bears the name of a President, but it almost didn't make it. The first name choice for that part of the Oregon Territory was "Columbia." It was changed to Washington after a brief consideration of "Washingtonia," a form thought to head off confusion with the national capital, Washington, D.C. Four state capitals are named after our Presidents — Jackson, Mississippi; Jefferson City, Missouri; Lincoln, Nebraska; and Madison, Wiscon-

sin. Anyone who tries to include Bismarck, North Dakota, is mixed up.

There are many counties, cities and towns, as well as physical features, named after our former Presidents. Some places like Cleveland, Ohio, and Ford City, Pennsylvania, are not named after Presidents. To see how our nation has viewed its Presidents in the placing of names across the fifty states, an exhaustive compilation of presidential place names has been put together.

Starting with the unabridged index of 110,000 place names in the HAMMOND MEDALLION ATLAS, we

have searched the records and cross-checked place name dictionaries to come up with our Presidential Preferential Geographical Naming Poll. Please note that all places which are "known" to be named after a President are noted as confirmed. Unconfirmed names include all those possibly or probably named for a President but precise information is lacking. Also note that names combining ville, park, burg, port, etc., are part of the tally, but that places named for persons with the same surname as Presidents are not counted.

Washington, George
State — Washington
Capital — Washington, D.C.
Counties — 31
Ala., Ark., Colo., Fla., Ga., Idaho, Ill., Ind., Iowa, Kansas, Ky., La., Maine, Md., Minn., Miss., Mo., Neb., N.C., N.Y., Ohio, Okla., Oreg., Pa., R.I., Tenn., Tex., Utah, Vt., Va., Wisc.
Cities and towns — 45
22 confirmed
23 unconfirmed
Other features
2 lakes — Fla., Wash.
1 mountain — N.H.
1 island — Wisc.

Jefferson, Thomas
Counties — 25
Ala., Ark., Colo., Fla., Ga., Idaho, Ill., Ind., Iowa, Kansas, Ky., La., Miss., Mo., Mont., Neb., N.Y., Ohio, Okla., Oreg., Pa., Tenn., Wash., W.Va., Wisc.
Cities and towns — 38
10 confirmed
28 unconfirmed
Other features
3 mountains — Nev., N.H., Oreg.
1 river — Mont.
1 national forest — Ky.-Va.

Jackson, Andrew
Counties — 21
Ala., Ark., Colo., Fla., Ill., Ind., Iowa, Kansas, Ky., La., Mich., Miss., Mo., N.C., Ohio, Okla., Oreg., Tenn., Tex., W.Va., Wisc.

Cities and towns — 36
14 confirmed
22 unconfirmed
Other features
1 mountain — Mont.
1 lake — Ga.

Madison, James
Counties — 20
Ala., Ark., Fla., Ga., Idaho, Ill., Ind., Iowa, Ky., La., Miss., Mo., Mont., Neb., N.Y., N.C., Ohio, Tenn., Tex., Va.
Cities and towns — 37
20 confirmed
17 unconfirmed
Other features
2 mountains —Mont., N.H.
1 plateau — Wyo.

Lincoln, Abraham
Counties — 18
Ark., Colo., Idaho, Kansas, La., Minn., Miss., Mont., Neb., Nev., N. Mex., Okla., Oreg., S. D., Wash., W.Va., Wisc., Wyo.
Cities and towns — 35
19 confirmed
16 unconfirmed
Other features
3 mountains — Colo., N.H., Vt.
1 mountain pass — Vt.

Monroe, James
Counties — 17
Ala., Ark., Fla., Ga., Ill., Ind., Iowa, Ky., Mich., Miss., Mo., N.Y., Ohio, Pa., Tenn., W.Va., Wisc.

Cities and towns — 33
14 confirmed
19 unconfirmed
Other features
2 mountains — N.H., Utah

Grant, Ulysses S.
Counties — 12
Ark., Kansas, La., Minn., Neb., N. Mex., N.D., Okla., Oreg., S.D., Wash., W.Va.
Cities and towns — 20
11 confirmed
9 unconfirmed
Other features
1 mountain range — Nev.

Polk, James
Counties — 11
Ark., Fla., Ga., Iowa, Minn., Mo., Neb., Oreg., Tenn., Texas, Wisc.
Cities and towns — 8
1 confirmed
7 unconfirmed

Adams, John
Counties — 8
Idaho, Iowa, Miss., Neb., Ohio, Pa., Wash., Wisc.
Cities and towns — 23
2 confirmed
21 unconfirmed
Other features
3 mountains — N.H., Utah, Wash.

Garfield, James
Counties — 6
Colo., Mont., Neb., Okla., Utah, Wash.

Cities and towns — 13
5 confirmed
8 unconfirmed
Other features
2 mountains — Colo., Idaho

Harrison, William Henry
Counties — 4
Ind., Iowa, Miss., Ohio
Cities and towns — 17
3 confirmed
14 unconfirmed

Taylor, Zachary
Counties — 4
Fla., Ga., Iowa, Ky.
Cities and towns — 14
3 confirmed
11 unconfirmed
Other features
2 mountains — Alaska, N. Mex.

Pierce, Franklin
Counties — 4
Ga., Neb., Wash., Wisc.
Cities and towns — 10
2 confirmed
8 unconfirmed
Other features
1 mountain — Calif.

Van Buren, Martin
Counties — 4
Ark., Iowa, Mich., Tenn.
Cities and towns — 7
4 confirmed
3 unconfirmed

Buchanan, James
Counties — 3
Iowa, Mo., Va.
Cities and towns — 7
2 confirmed
5 unconfirmed

Cleveland, Grover
Counties — 2
Ark., Okla.
Cities and towns — 17
2 confirmed
15 unconfirmed
Other features
1 mountain — Mont.
1 national forest — Calif.

Roosevelt, Theodore
Counties — 2
Mont., N. Mex.
Cities and towns — 10
10 unconfirmed
Other features
1 lake — Ariz.
1 national park — N. D.

Fillmore, Millard
Counties — 2
Minn., Neb.
Cities and towns — 8
1 confirmed
7 unconfirmed

Adams, John Quincy
Counties — 2
Ill., Ind.
Cities and towns
No known towns named after
    J.Q. Adams
Other features
1 mountain spur — N. 4.

Tyler, John
County — 1
Texas
Cities and towns — 10
10 unconfirmed

Hayes, Rutherford B.
County — 1
Neb.
Cities and towns — 7
1 confirmed
6 unconfirmed
Other features
1 mountain — N.H.

Arthur, Chester A.
County — 1
Neb.
Cities and towns — 8
1 confirmed
7 unconfirmed
Other features
1 mountain peak —Wyo.
1 lake — Pa.

McKinley, William
County — 1
N. Mex.
Cities and towns — 3
3 unconfirmed
Other features
1 mountain — Alaska

Harding, Warren
County — 1
N. Mex.
Other features
2 lakes — Ala., Ga.
1 icefield — Alaska

Taft, William Howard
Cities and towns — 5
3 confirmed
2 unconfirmed

Roosevelt, Franklin D.
Cities and towns — 3
3 confirmed

Wilson, Woodrow
Cities and towns — 2
2 unconfirmed
Other features
1 mountain — Wyo.
1 dam and reservoir — Ala.

Coolidge, Calvin
Cities and towns — 2
1 confirmed
1 unconfirmed
Other features
1 dam — Ariz.

Hoover, Herbert
Cities and towns — 2
2 unconfirmed
Other features
1 reservoir— Ohio
1 dam — Ariz.

Kennedy, John F.
Other features
1 International Airport

Reagan, Ronald
Other features
1 dam — Calif.

There are no counties, cities or towns or important places in the United States named after Presidents **Andrew Johnson, Benjamin Harrison, Truman, Eisenhower, Lyndon Johnson, Nixon, Ford** or **Carter.**

FORKS FIRST TO BECOME WASHINGTON?

Records indicate that the very first town in America to change its name to **Washington** in honor of **George** was the community of Forks of Tar River, North Carolina, which became Washington in 1775. It was not incorporated until April 13, 1782, however, so the town of Washington, Georgia, which incorporated January 23, 1780, is considered the first town to incorporate under the Washington name.

THE PRESIDENTS

On March 4, 1801, **Thomas Jefferson** walked the one block from Conrad's boardinghouse, where he was living, to the Capitol for his inauguration. This was the first presidential inauguration to take place in Washington, D. C.

HE LOOKS BETTER FROM A DISTANCE

Harry Truman's stature has grown greatly since the days of his presidency. During the Truman administration, the feeling of many was expressed by Martha, the wife of Senator Robert Taft, who said of the President, "To err is Truman."

THE FIRST

The first President to campaign by telephone was **William McKinley,** in 1896.

HE DIED WITH HIS QUOTES ON

Following his presidency, **John Quincy Adams** was elected to the House of Representatives from Massachusetts.

The only ex-President to serve as a Representative, he was a member of the House from 1830 to 1848.

Known as "Old Man Eloquent," the 80-year-old Adams was at his desk in the House when he suffered a stroke. He was taken to the Speaker's Office, where he died two days later, having regained consciousness only long enough to say, "Thank the officers of the House. This is the last of earth. I am content."

Which certainly was eloquent under the circumstances.

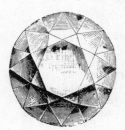

LOVE ME LONG

The President who enjoyed the longest marriage and, from all evidence, one of the happiest was **John Adams.** He was married to Abigail Smith on October 25, 1764, and the marriage lasted for over 54 years until death did them part.

Theodore Roosevelt's first marriage to Alice Lee, which lasted three years until her death at the age of 22, was the shortest presidential marriage.

Two years later, Roosevelt was married to Edith Carow; this marriage lasted for 32 years.

MY SON, MY SON

When John F. Kennedy, Jr., arrived, the first baby born to a President-elect, a reporter asked the new father, "Do you want your son to grow up to be President?"

Kennedy replied, "I just want him to be all right."

SUNLIGHT AND SHADOWS

Plus side:
  Oldest son of a President. Brilliant. Graduate of Harvard. Lawyer.

Minus side:
  Daydreamer. Unable to cope. Easily discouraged. Tended toward depression.

Suicide?
  Night of April 29, 1829. He took a steamer from Providence, Rhode Island, to New York City. Morning of April 30. He disappeared from the steamer. His body was found on City Island in lower Long Island Sound, east of the Bronx. He was 28.

His name:
  George Washington Adams, son of **John Quincy Adams.**

John Quincy Adams:
  Historical figure. Illustrious personage.

John Quincy Adams:
  Husband. Bereaved father. Just another one of us human beings.

FINIS

Tidbits & Trivia

WASN'T THAT A TASTY DISH TO SET BEFORE A PRESIDENT?

Whenever you pass a diner on the highway and see a number of trucks parked outside, you can be quite sure of one thing — a lot of truck drivers have eaten there. The same thing can be said of the White House. A lot of Presidents have eaten there.

Being a President no more qualifies a man to judge good food than being an athlete qualifies a man to judge shaving cream (or popcorn makers) in a TV commercial. Nor does a liking of good food necessarily qualify one to be a President. However, while our Presidents have certainly been more concerned with running the country than with eating, it is also certain that some among them have had a lively interest in food. The only trend in presidential preference seems to have been a liking for seafood and sweets.

These are recipes for dishes which are tasty and easy to prepare, and which happen to have been presidential favorites. More important, they have been selected for inclusion here by cooks who probably would have made terrible Presidents.

Try these recipes and enjoy them. May you eat and drink with more enthusiasm than James Madison and less enthusiasm than William Howard Taft.

THE PRESIDENTS

The Washingtons

The Chesapeake and its bounty were important to Washington's table at Mount Vernon, and Martha's way with crab soup has pleased even modern Presidents and their wives. While Martha boiled her own crabs for this dish, it is delicious with canned or frozen crab meat, and far easier.

MARTHA WASHINGTON'S CRAB SOUP

1 cup crab meat	Dash salt
1 tbsp butter	Dash pepper
1½ tbsp flour	4 cups milk
3 hard-boiled eggs, mashed with fork	½ cup heavy cream
	½ cup sherry
1 lemon rind, grated	Dash Worcestershire sauce

Combine butter, flour, mashed hard-boiled eggs, lemon rind, salt and pepper in a large pot. Bring to boil 4 cups milk, then pour slowly into butter and flour mixture. Add crab meat and cook at medium heat 5 minutes. Add cream, stir and remove from heat before soup reaches full boil. Add sherry and Worcestershire sauce. Serve very hot.

Makes 6 servings

Tidbits & Trivia

John and Abigail Adams

First to live in the White House, John and Abigail Adams opened the Executive Mansion to the public with a New Year's Day reception in 1801. On the menu that day was Floating Island, an eye-and-palate-pleasing pudding whose popularity has spanned the centuries.

FLOATING ISLAND

5 egg yolks
5 egg whites
1 quart milk
8 tbsp sugar

Dash of vanilla extract
  (optional)
⅛ tsp salt

Beat egg yolks together with one egg white. Scald milk and stir a little into the egg mixture to prevent curdling, then add rest of milk and 5 tablespoons of the sugar. Cook over low fire until thickened. Remove from heat, cool and flavor with vanilla if desired. Pour custard into bowl and chill. Add salt to remaining 4 egg whites and whip until frothy, adding remaining 3 tablespoons of sugar. Pour froth onto a shallow dish of boiling water to allow steam-cooking of meringue. When firm, drop by tablespoonsful on top of the custard far enough apart so that "islands" do not touch. Serve cold. You may also pour custard into individual cups, dropping an "island" on top of each.

Makes 6-8 servings

The Madisons

"Queen" Dolley, whose reputation as a hostess remains unchallenged by any other First Lady, reigned sixteen years in Washington, first as hostess to widower Thomas Jefferson, then eight more years during her husband's administration. The "Jefferson" soft gingerbread was a specialty from her famous kitchen.

SOFT GINGERBREAD

1 cup molasses
2/3 cup fresh beef drippings
1 rounded tsp baking soda
1/4 cup hot water
1 cup very hot water

2 1/4 cups flour
1 rounded tbsp ground ginger
1 tbsp ground cinnamon
Powdered sugar

Mix molasses and beef drippings; dissolve baking soda in the 1/4 cup of hot water and add to molasses and drippings mixture. Sift together flour, ginger and cinnamon and add alternately with the cup of very hot water to molasses and drippings mixture. Beat well until batter is thoroughly mixed and soft enough to pour. Bake in shallow, well-greased pan at 350° for 30 to 40 minutes, or until center of cake springs back when pressed gently. Serve warm, sprinkled with powdered sugar.

Makes 6 servings

Note: Dolley used New Orleans molasses. Lard flavored with a drop or two of beef extract may be substituted for the beef drippings.

The Lincolns

While historians generally agree that Lincoln took little notice of what he ate, he was known to praise his wife's baking and take particular pleasure in oysters served in a variety of ways. He enjoyed this recipe at his own table in Illinois, where oyster feasts were popular, and later at the White House.

SCALLOPED OYSTERS

¼ cup melted butter
2 cups coarse cracker
  crumbs
2 dozen oysters, drained
(reserve liquid)

¼ tsp coarse black pepper
⅓ cup cream
2 tbsp sherry
1 tsp Worcestershire sauce

Mix melted butter and cracker crumbs. Sprinkle a third of mixture evenly on bottom of greased, shallow baking dish and add layer of oysters. Stir together cream, oyster liquid, sherry, pepper and Worcestershire sauce; pour half of sauce mixture over oysters. Add one-third more of butter and crumb mixture to baking dish, place remaining oysters on top and add remaining sauce. Sprinkle rest of crumb mixture on top and bake at 425° for 10 or 15 minutes until crumbs are lightly browned.

Makes 6 servings

THE PRESIDENTS

The Grants and the Harrisons

President Grant's party libation is one of many Roman Punch recipes acclaimed over the years as White House thirst-quenchers.

ROMAN PUNCH

2 quarts lemonade, fresh or frozen concentrate
1 tbsp lemon extract

1 pint brandy
1 pint rum

Freeze lemonade to which lemon extract has been added. Just before serving, add brandy and rum to frozen mixture. Stir well; add ice if desired. Serve in tall glasses garnished with citrus fruit.

Makes 3 quarts
Note: Half lemonade and half orangeade may be used.

Caroline Harrison, our most domestic First Lady, gave the White House a thorough cleaning, started the china collection and compiled a cookbook, *Statesmen's Dishes and How to Cook Them* (1890). The recipes included this favorite which she served hot as an hors d'oeuvre or cold for a child's lunch-box treat.

SAUSAGE ROLLS

2 cups sifted flour
2½ tsp baking powder
1 tsp salt

¼ cup shortening
⅔ cup milk
Sausage, cut in pieces

Combine all ingredients except sausage to make light biscuit dough. Roll it out thin and cut into rounds with a biscuit cutter. Place small piece of browned sausage on dough, roll up dough to cover sausage and seal. Bake in a preheated oven at 450° for 10 to 15 minutes.

Makes 6 servings
Note: Caroline mixed her dough in the evening, let it rise overnight, and rolled it the following morning.

Tidbits & Trivia

The Roosevelts and the Tafts

The toothsome Sagamore Hill sweet is among a few favorite recipes that Edith Roosevelt jotted down and served to her lively family.

SAGAMORE HILL SAND TARTS

1 cup butter
2 cups sugar
3 eggs
  (separate white of one egg)

2 tsp vanilla
4 cups sifted flour
Cinnamon
Sugar

Cream together butter and sugar. Beat in eggs one by one and add vanilla. Add flour and mix well. Roll thin, cut into small cakes and brush surface of each with remaining egg white. Sprinkle with dash of cinnamon and pinch of sugar. Bake at 350° for 8 minutes.

Makes 6 dozen

Helen Taft, whose cherry-blossom legacy delights visitors to the Capital each spring, was as fond of the fruit as she was of the beautiful blooms. Her Spiced Cherries are an excellent accompaniment to poultry dishes.

SPICED CHERRIES

7 lbs sour red cherries
4 lbs sugar
1 quart vinegar

1 oz whole cloves
1 oz whole cinnamon

Alternate fruit and spices in layers in large kettle and let stand overnight. Boil sugar and vinegar together, then pour hot over fruit. Bring entire mixture to boil and cook one minute.

Makes 3½ quarts
Note: Damson plums may also be used in this recipe.

THE PRESIDENTS

The Wilsons and the Coolidges

This easy salad dressing was recorded by Edith Bolling Galt Wilson, who like the rest of the nation in wartime, observed meatless days at her table once each week.

QUICK FRENCH DRESSING

1 can tomato soup
1 cup tarragon vinegar
1 tbsp sugar

1 tbsp salt
1 onion, chopped
Olive oil

Dissolve sugar and salt in vinegar in 1-quart jar. Add tomato soup and onion. Fill jar almost to top with olive oil; shake thoroughly. Cover and refrigerate.

Makes about 1 quart

Note: White vinegar to which 1 tablespoon of tarragon has been added may be substituted. If a creamy French dressing is desired, prepare in electric blender.

Simple country fare like corn bread and custard pie were favorites of Vermonters "Silent Cal" and Grace. Fresh spinach, dressed up just a little, was often on their table, too.

SPINACH TIMBALES

1 cup chopped cooked
  spinach
½ tsp salt
1 tsp onion juice

1¼ cup milk
2 eggs, beaten
2 tbsp shortening
Dash pepper

Add salt, onion juice, eggs, milk and melted shortening to chopped spinach. Stir gently. Spoon into greased molds or custard cups set in pan of hot water. Line pan first with several thicknesses of brown paper. Bake at 350° for 30 to 35 minutes or until knife inserted in center of spinach molds comes out clean. Unmold and serve immediately.

Makes 4 servings

Tidbits & Trivia

The Hoovers and the Roosevelts

As Food Administrator during Wilson's administration, Herbert Hoover touted recipes like this 1918 War Bread which saved scarce commodities.

WAR BREAD

1 cup rye meal
1 cup graham flour
½ cup flour
1 tsp cream of tartar
1 tsp baking soda
1 tsp salt

¼ cup molasses
1 cup plus 3 tbsp sour milk
1 egg, well-beaten
2 tbsp melted shortening
½ cup raisins, chopped

Mix dry ingredients together. Add molasses, sour milk, egg, shortening and raisins and mix well. Bake in greased loaf pan in a preheated oven at 400° for 30 minutes.

Makes 1 loaf

Eleanor Roosevelt freely admitted she was not much of a cook, but her simple "chafing-dish scrambled eggs" suppers and timeless New England favorites like this Kedgeree were much enjoyed by family and friends.

KEDGEREE

2 cups cooked flaked
  seafood (white fish, crab
  meat, salmon, tuna, etc.)
2 cups cooked rice
½ cup milk or cream

4 tbsp melted butter
Dash salt
Dash pepper
4 hard-boiled eggs, sliced,
  chopped or quartered

Mix flaked fish and rice together, moistening with milk or cream. Sauté gently in melted butter. Add salt, pepper and hard-boiled eggs, and spoon fluffy mixture (do not pack down) into 1-quart casserole. Cook 15 minutes at 325° or until piping hot and slightly browned.

Makes 6 servings

THE PRESIDENTS

The Trumans

A great favorite with the White House staff, Bess Truman avoided the limelight, shining best herself at family meals with Harry and daughter Margaret. This simple but unusual dessert is one of the few recipes she has made public.

MRS. TRUMAN'S OZARK PUDDING

1 egg, well-beaten
¾ cup sugar
3 tbsp flour
1¼ tsp baking powder
⅛ tsp salt
1 tsp vanilla
½ cup chopped nuts
½ cup chopped pared apples

Add sugar gradually to well-beaten egg until mixture is very smooth. Sift flour, baking powder and salt, blend the dry ingredients into egg and sugar mixture and stir in vanilla. Fold in nuts and apples and stir well. Pour into buttered 9-inch pie plate or 1-quart casserole. Bake at 350° for 20 to 25 minutes. Serve with ice cream or whipped cream to which dash of sugar and 1 tablespoon of rum has been added.

Makes 6 servings

The Eisenhowers

Among Ike's own recipes, which sometimes took center stage when he and Mamie entertained, was this tasty beef stew. He enjoyed cooking it himself, even when making enough for sixty.

IKE'S BEEF STEW

2 lbs beef, cubed for stew
2 tbsp shortening
2 cans bouillon
1 can water
   Bouquet garni
12 small Irish potatoes, cut in half

1 bunch carrots, cut in 1-inch slices
12 white onions
2 large tomatoes cut in eighths
   Salt & Pepper
   Flour

Brown cubed beef in shortening, then add bouillon and water. Cover and simmer until beef is nearly tender. Add bouquet garni, potatoes, carrots, onions, tomatoes and salt and pepper to taste. Simmer about 20 minutes or until vegetables are tender. Remove bouquet garni and drain liquid into a saucepan. Using 2 tablespoons flour per cup of liquid, thicken gravy to medium consistency. Return gravy to stewpot and cook over low heat, stirring, until well thickened.

Makes 6 servings

Note: For bouquet garni, tie bay leaf, clove of garlic, parsley and thyme together in a cheesecloth bag.

THE PRESIDENTS

The Kennedys

His wife's preference for French cuisine was well known, but John Kennedy particularly liked this easy, tempting, shrimp and crab meat dish.

NEW ENGLAND SEAFOOD CASSEROLE

1 lb crab meat, canned, frozen or fresh-cooked, or use ½ lb lobster in place of half of the crab meat

1 lb shrimp, cooked and cleaned

½ cup chopped green pepper

¼ cup diced onion

1½ cups finely chopped celery

½ tsp salt

1 cup mayonnaise

1 tbsp Worcestershire sauce

2 cups crushed potato chips

1 tsp paprika

Combine all ingredients except potato chips and paprika and spoon into buttered 2-quart casserole dish. Top with potato chips and sprinkle with paprika. Bake in 400° oven 25 minutes or until hot and bubbly.

Makes 6 servings

The Johnsons

Lyndon and Lady Bird brought their own brand of Texas barbecue and other Southwestern specialties to the White House, among them this favorite recipe for chili.

PEDERNALES RIVER CHILI

4 lbs chuck, coarsely
    ground
2 small onions, chopped
2-3 cloves garlic, crushed
2 tsp salt
1 tsp oregano
1 tsp cumin seed

2 1-lb cans tomatoes,
    mashed slightly
2 tbsp chili powder
2 cups hot water
2 1-lb 4-oz cans kidney
    beans (optional)
2-6 dashes hot pepper sauce

Lightly brown beef, onions and garlic. Add salt, oregano, cumin seed, tomatoes and chili powder. Pour the hot water over all and mix thoroughly. Add kidney beans and/or hot sauce if desired. Simmer uncovered over low heat about an hour, skimming fat frequently. Serve hot at once, or store in refrigerator several days and reheat.

Makes 2½-3 quarts or 12 servings

THE PRESIDENTS

The Fords

Dressy and delicious, this spectacular strawberry dessert is a recipe Betty Ford takes pleasure in sharing.

STRAWBERRY BLITZ TORTE

1 cup sifted cake flour
1 tsp baking powder
¼ tsp salt
½ cup shortening
½ cup sugar
4 egg yolks
3 tbsp milk
1 tsp vanilla

Meringue:
4 egg whites
½ tsp salt
½ tsp cream of tartar
1 cup sugar
½ tsp vanilla
Strawberry filling:
½ cup whipping cream
2 tbsp confectioners' sugar
1 cup sliced strawberries

Sift flour, baking powder and salt three times. Combine shortening and sugar slowly, creaming mixture until light and fluffy. Beat egg yolks until thick and add to creamed mixture. Stir in milk and vanilla. Add dry ingredients and beat until smooth. Spread in two greased 8-inch layer cake pans. For meringue: Beat egg whites, salt and cream of tartar until they stand in peaks. Add sugar 2 tablespoons at a time, beating thoroughly after each addition. Add vanilla. Lightly pile half of the meringue mixture over batter in each pan. Bake in a preheated oven at 350° about 35 minutes. Remove from oven, loosen sides of tortes from pans and remove to wire racks, meringue-side-up. When cool, spread strawberry filling between the layers.
Strawberry filling: Combine whipping cream and confectioners' sugar; whip until stiff. Fold in sliced strawberries; spread between layers of Blitz Torte.

Makes one 2-layer cake

The Carters

Jimmy and Rosalynn Carter's warm, informal brand of Southern hospitality caught on quickly in Washington and across the country, where grits and other "down home" dishes were sampled and newly appreciated. The lowly peanut, however, symbol of Carter's business success, enjoyed the biggest boost in popularity.

Rich and creamy, this peanut soup, a favorite recipe of Mrs. Carter's, is deliciously worthy of the White House table.

PEANUT SOUP

¼ cup minced onion
1 tbsp butter or
  margarine
½ cup smooth peanut
  butter

1 can (10½ oz.) cream
  of chicken soup
2 soup cans milk
¼ cup chopped peanuts
  (optional)

Melt butter and sauté onion in it until transparent and soft (do not brown). Stir in peanut butter, and when heated through, blend in soup and milk gradually. Add chopped, salted peanuts if desired. Stir until smooth and heat until just before boiling. (Do not boil.) Serve at once, garnished with additional chopped peanuts, parsley or dash of paprika.

Makes 4-6 servings

THE PRESIDENTS

FOR FURTHER READING ON THE PRESIDENTS

George Washington
Flexner, James T., *Washington: The Indispensable Man*. Little, Brown & Co., Boston, 1974.

Freeman, Douglas S., *George Washington: A Biography*. 7 volumes, (1948-1957). Reprinted by Augustus M. Kelley, Publishers, Fairfield, N.J., 1975.

John Adams
Smith, Page, *John Adams*. 2 volumes, 1962. Reprinted by Greenwood Press, Inc., Westport, Conn.

Thomas Jefferson
Malone, Dumas, *Jefferson and His Time*. 5 volumes. Little, Brown & Co., Boston, 1948-1974.

Schachner, Nathan, *Thomas Jefferson: A Biography*. A.S. Barnes & Co., Inc., Cranbury, N.J., 1951.

James Madison
Brant, Irving, *The Fourth President: The Life of James Madison*. Bobbs-Merrill Co., Indianapolis, 1956.

James Monroe
Cresson, William P., *James Monroe*. (1946). Reprinted by Shoe String Press, Inc., Hamden, Conn., 1971.

John Quincy Adams
Nevins, Allan, ed., *The Diary of John Quincy Adams, 1794-1845*. (1951). Reprinted by Frederick Ungar Publishing Co., New York, 1969.

Andrew Jackson
Schlesinger, Arthur M., Jr., *The Age of Jackson*. Little, Brown & Co., Boston, 1945.

Van Deusen, Glyndon G., *The Jacksonian Era*. Harper & Row, New York, 1959.

Martin Van Buren
Remini, R. V., *Martin Van Buren and the Making of the Democratic Party*. Columbia University Press, New York, 1959.

William H. Harrison
Cleaves, Freeman, *Old Tippecanoe*. (1939). Reprinted by Kennikat Press, Port Washington, N.Y., 1969.

John Tyler
Chitwood, Oliver P., *John Tyler, Champion of the Old South*. (1939). Revised edition by Russell & Russell, Publishers, New York, 1964.

Seager, Robert, *And Tyler Too*. McGraw-Hill Inc., New York, 1963.

James K. Polk
Gerson, Noel B., *The Slender Reed*. Doubleday & Co., Garden City, N.Y., 1965.

Zachary Taylor
Hoyt, Edwin P., *Zachary Taylor*. Reilly & Lee Co., Chicago, 1966.

Millard Fillmore
Rayback, Robert J., *Millard Fillmore: Biography of a President*. Henry Stewart, Inc., East Aurora, N.Y., 1959.

Franklin Pierce
Nichols, Roy F., *Franklin Pierce, Young Hickory of the Granite Hills*. (1958). Revised edition, University of Pennsylvania Press, University Park, Pa., 1964.

James Buchanan
Klein, Philip S., *President James Buchanan: A Biography*. Pennsylvania State University Press, University Park, Pa., 1962.

Abraham Lincoln
Sandburg, Carl, *Abraham Lincoln: The Prairie Years and the War Years*. (Revised ed.) Harcourt, Brace and Company, New York, 1954.

Thomas, Benjamin P., *Abraham Lincoln*. Alfred A. Knopf, Inc., New York, 1952.

Andrew Johnson
Winston, Robert W., *Andrew Johnson: Plebian and Patriot*. (1928). Reprinted by AMS Press, Inc., New York, 1970.

Ulysses S. Grant
Catton, Bruce, *U.S. Grant and the American Military Tradition*. Little, Brown & Co., Boston, 1954.

Hesseltine, William B., *Ulysses S. Grant: Politician*. (1935). Reprinted by Frederick Ungar Publishing Co., New York.

Rutherford B. Hayes
Bernard, Harry, *Rutherford B. Hayes and His America*. Russell & Russell, Publishers, 1954.

James A. Garfield
Severn, Bill, *Teacher, Soldier, President: The Life of James A. Garfield*. Ives Washburn, Inc., New York, 1964.

Chester A. Arthur
Howe, George Frederick, *Chester A. Arthur: A Quarter Century of Machine Politics*. (1934). Reprinted by Frederick Ungar Publishing Co., New York.

Grover Cleveland
Nevins, Allan, *Grover Cleveland: A Study in Courage*. Dodd, Mead & Co., New York, 1932.

Benjamin Harrison
Sievers, Harry J., *Benjamin Harrison: Hoosier Statesman*. 2 volumes. Bobbs-Merrill Co., Indianapolis, 1952, 1959.

William McKinley
Leach, Margaret, *In the Days of McKinley*. Harper & Row, New York, 1959.

Theodore Roosevelt
Mowry, George E., *The Era of Theodore Roosevelt, 1900-1912*. Harper & Row, New York, 1958.

Wagenknecht, Edward C., *The Seven Worlds of Theodore Roosevelt*. Longmans, Green, 1958.

William H. Taft
Pringle, Henry F., *The Life and Times of William Howard Taft*. 2 volumes. Farrar & Rinehart, Inc., New York, 1939.

Woodrow Wilson
Link, Arthur S., *Woodrow Wilson and the Progressive Era*. Harper & Row, New York, 1954.

Walworth, Arthur, *Woodrow Wilson*. 2 volumes, 3rd ed W. W. Norton & Co., New York, 1978.

Warren G. Harding
Russell, Francis, *The Shadow of Blooming Grove: Warren G. Harding in His Times*. McGraw-Hill Book Co., New York, 1968.

Calvin Coolidge
Fuess, Claude M., *Calvin Coolidge, The Man from Vermont*. (1940). Reprinted by Greenwood Press, Inc., Westport, Conn., 1977.

Herbert Hoover
Warren, Harris G., *Herbert Hoover and the Great Depression*. (1959). Revised edition, W. W. Norton & Co., New York, 1967.

Franklin D. Roosevelt
Burns, James MacGregor, *Roosevelt: The Soldier of Freedom*. Harcourt Brace Jovanovich, Inc., New York, 1970.

Gunther, John, *Roosevelt in Retrospect*. Harper & Row, New York, 1950.

Schlesinger, Arthur M., Jr., *The Age of Roosevelt*. 2 volumes. Houghton Mifflin Co., Boston, 1957, 1960.

Harry S Truman
Miller, Merle, *Plain Speaking*. Berkeley Publishing Corp., New York 1974.

Phillips, Cabell, *The Truman Presidency*. Macmillan Co., New York, 1966.

Dwight D. Eisenhower
Eisenhower, Dwight D., *The White House Years*. 2 volumes. Doubleday & Co., Garden City, N.Y., 1963, 1965.

John F. Kennedy
Schlesinger, Arthur M., Jr., *A Thousand Days: John F. Kennedy In The White House*. Houghton Mifflin Co., Boston, 1965.

Sorensen, Theodore C., *Kennedy*. Harper & Row, New York, 1965.

Wicker, Tom, *JFK and LBJ*. Pelican Publishing Co., Gretna, La., 1968.

Lyndon B. Johnson
Geyelin, Philip L., *Lyndon B. Johnson and the World*. Praeger, New York, 1966.

Kearns, Doris, *Lyndon Johnson and the American Dream*. Harper & Row, New York, 1976.

Richard M. Nixon
Mazo, Earl, & Hess, Stephen, *Nixon: A Political Portrait*. Harper & Row, New York, 1968.

Nixon, Richard M., *RN: The Memoirs of Richard Nixon*. Grosset & Dunlap, Inc., New York, 1978.

—, *Six Crises*. Doubleday & Co., Garden City, N.Y., 1962.

White, Theodore, *Breach of Faith: The Fall of Richard Nixon*. Atheneum, New York, 1975.

Gerald R. Ford
Ter Horst, Jerald F., *Gerald Ford: Past ... Present ... Future*. Third Press — Joseph Okpaku Publishing Co., New York, 1974.

James E. Carter
Glad, Betty, *Jimmy Carter: From Plains to The White House*. W. W. Norton & Co., New York, 1978.

Mercer, Charles, *Jimmy Carter*. G. P. Putnam's Sons, New York, 1977.

Wooten, James, *Dasher: The Roots & Rising of Jimmy Carter*. Summit Books, New York, 1978.

Ronald Reagan
Boyarsky, Bill, *Ronald Reagan: His Life and Rise to the Presidency*. Random House, New York, 1981.

Reagan, Ronald & Hubler, Richard G., *Where's the Rest of Me?* Karz Pub., New York, 1965 reprint.

INDEX

160